Romans & Reconciliation:
The Message of Romans for the Trenches

Randy Colver

Romans and Reconciliation: The Message of Romans for the Trenches
Copyright © 2006, 2009, 2010 by Randy Colver
All rights reserved. Third Edition.

ISBN 978-1-84728-221-7

Scripture taken from the HOLY BIBLE,
NEW INTERNATIONAL VERSION®.
NIV®. Copyright © 1973, 1978, 1984, by International Bible Society.
Used by permission of Zondervan Publishing House. All rights reserved.

Contents

Introduction	v
1 Introduction, Purpose, and Background	1
2 The Judaizer Threat	11
3 Paul at a Crossroads	15
4 The Greater Purpose of Reconciliation	19
5 Equal Basis Theology	25
6 Reconciliation in the Broader Context of the NT	33
7 Paul's Core Values	41
8 Our Relationship to the Law	43
9 The Core of Paul's Theology	49
10 Christ Event Mapping to Our Lives	53
11 What about Israel?	55
12 Contemporary Relevance – Racial Reconciliation	59
13 Paul's Character	63
Appendix A: Overview	76
Appendix B: Background	75
Appendix C: The Law	79
Appendix D: Principles	83
Appendix E: Christ Event	88
Appendix F: God's Plan	99
Appendix G: The Jew/Gentile Racial Setting of the NT	105
Bibliography	121
Index of Scripture Verses	125

Introduction

AFRICAN AMERICANS should "own" Romans. Unfortunately, like most of us, they were taught that Paul wrote Romans as a compendium of theology. But if its overall purpose had been understood, that is, if Paul's purpose for reconciling Jewish and Gentile Christians had been taught as its overall message, one wonders if the problem of racism in the Church of America would exist as it does today.

Not too long ago, and with penetrating clarity of conscience, the Reverend Martin Luther King, Jr., exposed Sunday mornings as the most segregated time of the week. Has this really changed? Or have we simply accepted the status quo? Only a few scattered multi-racial churches exist in Atlanta. Even in these we can find segregation just below the surface—in leadership, friendships, and small group meetings.

But could it be that God's answer for reconciliation lies written before us all the time? What if the problems in the first-century Church in many ways match the problems of today? What if the solutions to those problems—at least in principle—still apply today? Could we not find powerful truths to deal with racism, especially for the Church?

"Romans and Reconciliation: The Message of Romans for the Trenches" seeks to provide a unique perspective on Paul's message to the Romans and apply it to the practical needs of the Church today—especially in the area of reconciliation. Without sacrificing theology (wherein Paul actually provides the keys to overcoming racism), this little book offers practical advice from the words of Scripture.

I am not alone on this—many scholars maintain this same perspective on Romans. Unfortunately, this message has remained largely in the sphere of scholarly debate, papers, and commentaries. Rarely has it reached the trenches.

While accessible to the average reader, I have chosen to write this primarily to help teachers and pastors, who are really the ones who disseminate truth to the average member. Further, anyone who has a passion to teach knows the value of good classroom material. Unfortunately, teachers frequently spend hours gleaning from many sources to prepare actual class notes and assignments. By writing "Romans and Reconciliation" I hope to provide teachers with a complete and ready source of class lectures, assignments, and presentations for classroom use. I recommend it for adult Bible study, or for students at an undergraduate level, as an introduction, although its contents often go much deeper than surface issues. The footnotes contain many insights for further study and some important Greek words or phrases.

This work reflects the culmination of years of study, research, writing and teaching Romans. Logos Christian College used a preceding workbook version, and I incorporated a paper I presented at the 51st Annual Meeting of the Evangelical Theological Society into the present contents. The first, and major, section gives the class lecture notes, as well as the references to the presentations located in the Appendix section of the book.

"Romans and Reconciliation" centers on the message of the book of Romans as a whole, rather than (as is most often done) using it as a launching pad for topical study. I've tried to balance theology with "practicology" throughout, and break up the lecture with hands-on assignments and presentations.

Teachers may prefer to distribute the book to each student in class as they will benefit from having the notes and following along. To help students follow the lecture notes, I divided the ideas into chapters and added paragraph numbering.

For teachers, I recommend keeping the commentaries by the "3Ms" always close at hand—Murray, Morris, and Moo, and one should read the sections about Romans in Longnecker's "Paul, Apostle of Liberty," Bruce's "Paul, Apostle of the Heart Set Free," and Schreiner's "Paul, Apostle of God's Glory in Christ." The best, however, especially for pre-class review, is Donfried's "The

Romans Debate," which should get marked up, dog-eared, and post-it note cluttered. (To those who think I should have included a bibliography, I just did. Besides, real teachers check the footnotes!)

I need to acknowledge my editor, Dale Glass-Hess, who deserves much more credit than he gets. And I'd like to say, "Hi mom!" because she put up with me for so many years.

May your days of teaching Paul's epistle to the Romans be as rewarding as mine have.

—the Author

> "We rejoice in God through our Lord Jesus Christ, through whom we have now received reconciliation."
> —Romans 5:11

1

Introduction, Purpose, and Background

1. WHAT ARE YOUR FAVORITE VERSES IN ROMANS? Perhaps, like many who have enjoyed this enduring letter, you would choose Romans 8:28: "And we know that in all things God works for the good of those who love him, who have been called according to his purpose," or perhaps Romans 8:31: "If God is for us who can be against us." Recalling what you know about Romans, can you think of a verse (or verses) that really sums up the purpose of Romans? Look at Romans 1:14-17. Many Bible expositors believe that Paul summarizes his purpose—at least a very important part of it—in these verses. What important truths do you see in these verses? Not only does Paul make opening statements about the gospel, righteousness, salvation, and faith, but he also adds that *everyone* may obtain salvation: "first for the Jew, then for the Gentile" (Ro. 1:16). Why would he specifically use these terms? Are they important for what Paul wants to say? Are they important for us today?

2. What do you see in Romans as a whole? What has the book meant to you? For many years Bible expositors viewed Paul's Epistle to the Romans as a compendium of theology. While Romans certainly contains much theology, Paul wrote the epistle for a special people living in a special set of circumstances. Just like Paul's other epistles *without exception,*

Introduction, Purpose, and Background

this one is thoroughly ad hoc. Further, if Paul intended Romans as a compendium, then why does he omit the important theological doctrine of communion, for example?

3. Before we discover the complete answer to Paul's purpose, let's briefly overview the book itself. Romans 1:1-17 and 15:14-33 frames the epistle with Paul's explanation for writing it. The body of the letter contains a lengthy discussion, both theological (Ro. 1:18-11:36) and paraenetical[1] (containing practical exhortations and axioms, Romans 12:1-15:13), with Paul's personal greetings following in Romans 16. We should also note that in chapter three Paul poses a series of questions which he answers later in the letter. Thus, this chapter sets the stage for the ensuing theological discussions. To wit, we find here the summary statement from which Paul's theology will follow:

> But now a righteousness from God, apart from law, has been made known, to which the Law and the Prophets testify. This righteousness from God comes through faith in Jesus Christ to all who believe. There is no difference, for all have sinned and fall short of the glory of God, and are justified freely by his grace through the redemption that came by Christ Jesus. God presented him as a sacrifice of atonement, through faith in his blood. He did this to demonstrate his justice, because in his forbearance he had left the sins committed beforehand unpunished—he did it to demonstrate his justice at the present time, so as to be just and the one who justifies those who have faith in Jesus. Where, then, is boasting? It is excluded. On what principle? On that of observing the law? No, but on that of faith. For we maintain that a man is justified by faith apart from observing the law. Is God the God of Jews only? Is he not the God of Gentiles too? Yes, of Gentiles too, since there is only one God, who will justify the circumcised by faith and

---

[1] See Romans 14:1-15:13, which contains thirteen imperatives. Paul begins this section (Ro. 12:1) with his characteristic "parakalo," "I beseech."

the uncircumcised through that same faith.—Romans 3:21-30

Is Paul's theological emphasis righteousness by faith apart from the law? Some have thought so. Paul clearly makes this a major theme. But so is justification by grace in contrast to observing the law. Still, one could make a case that the "sacrifice of atonement, through faith in his blood" embodies the core of Paul's theology.

However, if we focus only on theology, we will miss the fact that Paul couches all his theological discussion in terms of the Jew/Gentile situation. In other words, Paul directs his theology to answer specific needs at Rome.

Donald Madvig quotes William Lane as asserting:

> The context in which Paul introduces the concept of the righteousness of God is the most striking feature of his exposition. Every passage in which Paul speaks of righteousness occurs within a larger context discussing the relationship of Jews and Gentiles in the one church of Christ. In each instance they illustrate the thoroughly missionary character of Romans. Paul's teaching on justification by faith is best understood as the answer to a persistent question: How is it possible for the Jew and the Gentile to stand on the same level of advantage before God?[2]

4. Was there a situation at Rome that would explain all the pieces of the book, e.g., practical, theological, and situational? Why does the book contain lengthy discussions on the equality of Jews and Gentiles in Christ (Ro. 2-3) and admonitions for each group not to boast (e.g., Ro. 3:27, 11:17-20)? What is meant by Paul's gospel and the "end of the law" (Ro. 10:4), and what is the purpose of the Jews and their election (Ro. 9-11)? Does any

---

[2] G. W. Baker, W. L. Lane and J. R. Michaels, *The New Testament Speaks* (New York, 1969) 192. Cited in D. Madvig, *The Missionary Preaching of Paul: A Problem in New Testament Theology,* **Journal of the Evangelical Theological Society**, vol. 20, no. 2, 1977, 150.

Introduction, Purpose, and Background

one situation or problem answer Paul's practical admonitions in Romans 12 and 14? Who are the "weak" and the "strong" (Ro. 14)? What about obeying the Roman authorities and paying taxes in chapter 13? Why were there so many house churches that seem to be divided between Jews and Gentiles (Ro. 16)?[3]

5. The answer may lie in the background situation of the epistle. Let's look closely at the clues in Romans 15:23ff, Acts 18:2 and Romans 16:3-5. Emperor Claudius, according to Roman historian Seutonius, expelled the entire community of the Jews and Jewish Christians (some 40,000 people or more) in AD 49 from Rome! Evidently, he based this drastic decision on riots instigated by one "Chresto," probably an alternative reading for "Christo," a reference to Christ. Since there was no one leader over all the synagogue, Claudius may have felt compelled to expel the whole lot of them.[4]

Not long after this, Nero succeeded Claudius as the Roman emperor in AD 54. At this change in emperorship the edict would no longer be in force and these Jews could return to Rome without hindrance. Thus, the Bible records in Acts 18:2 that the Jewish Christian, Aquila, was expelled from Rome. Later we find him back in Rome (Ro. 16:3) when Paul wrote his letter to the Romans.

6. Now consider the Jewish situation at Rome. As the gospel spread around the Mediterranean world, it usually took root in the synagogues among Jews first, and Rome would be no exception. This means that most Christian worship would have followed many Jewish customs. (In fact, Roman leaders considered Christianity a sect of Judaism.) It follows that Jewish Christians most likely maintained their leadership and

---

[3] For example, Andronicus and Junias (Ro. 16:7), (probably) Aristobulus (Ro. 16:10), Prisca (Ro. 16:3; Acts 18:2, though Paulinist), and Herodian (Ro. 16:11) are Jews, the others are most likely Gentiles. The fact that Paul greets both groups as common friends is in itself reconciling.

[4] Shortly thereafter, Paul may have felt the impact of the edict indirectly while in Thessalonica (Acts 17:6f).

authority as custodians of the law and as progeny of the Patriarchs.

We know from Roman records that disturbances within the Jewish community (sparked by those opposed to the gospel?) resulted in an expulsion of their entire community from Rome. However, this expulsion would not have included the Gentile Christian population, who would naturally assume leadership responsibilities in the absence of the Jews. Almost overnight, the Gentile Christians became the majority at Rome and were responsible for its growth—even its very existence—at Rome.

Unlike the Jews, who are of "weaker conscience," Gentiles have little need or constraint to follow the legalistic customs of the Jewish Christians. Since the synagogues were either closed or likely off limits, they met in homes for worship. Soon, the whole face of Christianity in Rome became "Gentile."

A few years later, Emperor Claudius passed away and the expulsion decree became null and void. What would happen when the Jewish Christians returned? Would they be angry at their Gentile Christian brothers for spoiling things? Would they demand to worship differently or separately? Would they be antagonistic toward the Roman government for bringing the hardships of relocation upon them?

7. What would you do to solve this situation? Supposing you were Paul and wanted to have a clear base of operations for future missions endeavors into Spain (Ro. 15:23-28). Yet you knew that the Christian communities were divided largely between Jewish and Gentile Christians (the "weak" and the "strong"). How would you reconcile them? Would you try to bring them together? How would you do that? Would you try to get them to see eye-to-eye?

Introduction, Purpose, and Background

8. The point is that Paul dealt with present and potential division between the two groups[5] at Rome by seeking to unify the Jewish and Gentile Christians. He wanted to bring them together in fellowship, to overcome suspicion and racial differences, and worship together (Ro. 15:7ff). Paul did this by addressing each group in turn, leveling the playing field, and giving them practical admonitions for unity.

For example, note how Paul encourages unity through hospitality: "Accept [or welcome] one another, then, just as Christ accepted you, in order to bring praise to God. For I tell you that Christ has become a servant of the Jews on behalf of God's truth, to confirm the promises made to the patriarchs so that the Gentiles may glorify God for his mercy" (Ro. 15:7-8). Paul then follows this admonition with four Old Testament quotations regarding unity of Jews and Gentiles.

In addition, can it be that Paul speaks favorably toward the Jews (and Jewish Christians) "precisely so that the Gentile Christians would resist the temptation to join in the current slanderous anti-Jewish sentiment"[6] left over from their expulsion? Likewise, can it be that "Gentile Christians, far from feeling superior, should understand that what is happening with them is in the service of the salvation of Israel?"[7] (Ro. 11:11-25).

---

[5] Not counting the substitute terms such as "weak" and "strong," Paul uses the term "Jew" (or "Jews") fourteen times and the term "Gentile" (or "Gentiles") twenty-eight times in his epistle.

[6] Karl Donfried, *False Presuppositions in the Study of Romans*, in Karl Donfried, editor, *The Romans Debate* (Peabody: Hendrickson Publishers, 1991) 105.

[7] Loyd Gaston, *Israel's Misstep in the Eyes of Paul*, in *The Romans Debate*, 321.

Teaching Ideas

Show chapters 20 and 21 from the "The Bible Collection" DVD "Paul the Apostle." These scenes present the meeting of Paul with Priscilla and Aquila.

Use the Handout and the presentation steps in Appendix A to create a presentation as an overview of Romans. You can use this as a white board or PowerPoint presentation.

9. For our thesis to have merit, it must fit within the broader context of the epistle and especially occur at the turning points of Paul's argument. We've already noted that Paul includes the Jew/Gentile situation in Romans 1:14-17, where he establishes his theme. Whereas the meaning of the phrase "first for the Jew, then for the Gentile"[8] loses its importance for most readers today, the phrase is not an intrusion into the text; rather, it is central to the purpose of the epistle. Paul knows very well that the Jewish world view divides Jew from Gentile and that the situation at Rome exacerbates the separation of Jewish and Gentile Christians. Here, in his pivotal, opening remarks, Paul speaks to these directly, and then repeats the phrase twice more in Romans 2:9-10, concluding that "God does not show favoritism."

Similarly, we have already discussed how Paul's great statements on justification, righteousness, the atonement, and faith in Romans 3:21-30 all lead up to the concluding questions of Paul: "Is God the God of Jews only? Is he not the God of Gentiles too? Yes, of Gentiles too, since there is only one God, who will justify the circumcised by faith and the uncircumcised through that same faith" (Ro. 3:29-30). Paul directs his theology to the fact that we all—Jew and Gentile—receive these great blessings the same way—strictly by faith. Thus, no one has room to boast.

---

[8] Ἰουδαίῳ τε πρῶτον καὶ Ἕλληνι.

To level the ground, Paul shows how we are all guilty before God (Ro. 1:18-2:1, 12-16). He calls his review and indictment of humankind's sin a "charge:" "We have already made the charge that Jews and Gentiles alike are all under sin" (Ro. 3:9). He uses a forensic term here,[9] to "charge" or "accuse," to illustrate that we are all guilty before the court of heaven (Ro. 3:19). Paul's question may very well be translated, "Do we have a defense?" The answer is a resounding "No!" We all have the guilty indictment of sin charged against us.

In chapters six to eight, Paul again examines this universality of sin but now balances it with the universal release from condemnation (Ro. 8:1) of those in Christ and concludes: "Who will bring any charge against those whom God has chosen? It is God who justifies. Who is he that condemns? (Ro. 8:33-34a)."

At the critical juncture between the (basically) theological and pareanetical sections of Romans, Paul summarizes his theme (Ro. 11:25-26, 32). Again, at the end of his exhortations he summarizes the theme once more:

> "For I tell you that Christ has become a servant of the Jews on behalf of God's truth, to confirm the promises made to the patriarchs so that the Gentiles may glorify God for his mercy..."—Ro. 15:8

Thus, Paul gives us a central basis of relationship: we are equally unrighteous in Adam and equally righteous in Christ; therefore we all come to Christ the same way, whether Jew of Gentile. We will call this "equal basis theology" (and develop this further in Chapter 4).

---

[9] προητιασάμεθα. On the subject of the meaning of προεχόμεθα and Paul's question, see the discussion in W. Arndt and F. W. Gingrich, translators, W. Bauer, *A Greek-English Lexicon of the New Testament and Other Early Christian Literature* (Chicago: University of Chicago Press, 1957) 712, n. 2.

10. This brings us back to point #4 above. Do the background of the letter and our explanation of its purpose answer each of the questions we raised? Let's look at one more important piece before we answer this.

Teaching Idea

Do a class exercise. Divide the class into small groups. Read through Galatians and Ephesians to identify any remarks regarding the Jew/Gentile relationship.[10] Record your observations.

---

[10] Significant passages should include Gal. 1:11-5:14; 6:11-16; and Eph. 2:11-3:12.

Introduction, Purpose, and Background

2

The Judaizer Threat

1. SINCE THE NEW TESTAMENT EPISTLES are rooted in historical circumstances, let's look at the background of the epistle to the Romans from another direction. A group, comprised largely of Jewish Christians, and known derogatively to Paul as the Judaizers,[11] taught the necessity of keeping the Law of Moses and Jewish customs before becoming a Christian. The hallmarks of their heresy consisted of requiring circumcision (Gal. 5:2, 11; 6:12-15), separation from Gentiles (Gal. 2:14-21), observance of the Mosaic Law (Gal. 3:2; 5:4) and certain festivals (Gal. 4:10), and apparent interest in being 'sons of Abraham' (3:6-29; 4:21-31)."[12] In Jerusalem, the Judaizers consisted of a small, but vocal minority of Pharisees (Acts 15:5), who were known for their strict adherence to the law.

2. F. F. Bruce captured the argument well:

Their argument may well have run along these lines: "Paul has no authority of his own, no gospel of his own, apart from what he has received from Jerusalem. But he has not given you the whole Jerusalem gospel. The Jerusalem believers, with their leaders, revere the Law of Moses; every man among them has been circumcised. Of course they did not receive circumcision when they accepted Jesus as the Messiah, because they were

---

[11] The name "Judaizers" is taken from Gal. 2:14 (ioudaizo).
[12] Walt Russel, *Who Were Paul's Opponents in Galatia?*, **Bibliotheca Sacra**, vol. 147 #587, July 1990, 331.

circumcised already. But you were uncircumcised when you believed the gospel; if you are to be on the same footing as the Jerusalem Christians and to be acknowledged by them as fellow-heirs of salvation, fellow-members of the people of God, you must be circumcised too. If Paul told you otherwise, he had no authority to do so. His gospel is all right so far as it goes, but it is defective: be ruled by us, and have the deficiencies made good at once."[13]

3. Theologically, the heresy was a threat to the truth of the gospel (Gal. 2:14-16) because justification comes by faith alone (Gal. 2:15-21). In practical terms, it instilled a sectarian spirit by separating Jews from Gentiles and by pressuring Gentile Christians to conform to the customs of Judaism, especially if they wanted to have fellowship with the apostles (Gal. 2:14b).

4. Note the controversy that erupted when the Judaizers came to Antioch and taught that a person must first become a Jew before becoming a follower of Christ (Acts 15:1-2). At stake was not only how the gospel was to be presented to the Gentiles—would they have to jump through all the hoops of Judaism?—but the very gospel itself, which is not dependent on works (Eph. 2:8-10). The disagreement between Paul and the Judaizers resulted in the meeting at Jerusalem with the apostles and elders (Acts 15). The conclusion of the council sought to respect both Jews and Gentiles, thus preventing any hindrance for members of either group to come to Christ (Acts 15:19-21). Note how the spread of the gospel among both Jews and Gentiles is taken into account and balanced, especially with respect to the sensibilities of the Jews (the ones with the "weaker" conscience).[14]

---

[13] F. F. Bruce, *Paul, Apostle of the Heart Set Free* (Grand Rapids: Eerdmans, 1995) 180-181. See also an excellent assessment in Paul Minear, The Obedience of Faith (Eugene: Wipf and Stock Publishers, 1971) 73-74.

[14] The other commitment made by Paul at the Jerusalem council was to "remember the poor" (Gal. 2:20). Out of this request came Paul's passion to gather an offering from the Gentiles to the Jewish poor in Jerusalem. See Acts 24:17; Ro. 15:26; 1 Cor. 16:3-4; and 2 Cor. 8-9.

5. The heresy of the Judaizers worked against the reconciling nature of the gospel. Christ's very commission sought to "make disciples of all nations" (Mt. 28:19; cf. Acts 1:8[15]); and Paul stated that Christ "himself is our peace, who has made the two [Jews and Gentiles] one and has destroyed the barrier, *the dividing wall of hostility*" (Eph. 2:14). Hostility already existed between Jews and Gentiles in general (Eph. 2:11-22)[16] and the merging of dissimilar cultures and backgrounds would naturally cause friction and inevitably raise "questions as to Jewish and Christian identity."[17] This could be fuel for the Judaizer's match, and Paul sought to avoid disunity through the reconciliatory message of the gospel.

6. Paul had to deal with the sectarian spirit of the Judaizers on previous occasions: Gal. 2:11-21. They seemed to hound him like hyenas nipping at the heels of a lion with the prize in its teeth. A decade or so after the Jerusalem council's decision, Paul had harsh words for the Judaizers who had evidently influenced the Philippians by their heresy (Phil 3:2-4; cf. Gal. 5:12). Paul derided the Judaizers as the "concision"—mutilators of the flesh (Phil. 3:2).

---

[15] On the ethnic significance of Acts 1:8, see Thomas Moore, *"To the End of the Earth": The Geographical and Ethnic Universalism of Acts 1:8 in Light of Isaianic Influence on Luke*, **Journal of the Evangelical Theological Society** 40/3 (September 1997) 389-399. The mission to the Gentiles can also be seen in Christ's prediction of Matthew 10:18 and 24:9.

[16] τὴν ἐχθραν. See Bruce W. Fong, *Addressing the Issue of Racial Reconciliation According to the Principles of Ephesians 2:11-22*, **Journal of the Evangelical Theological Society**, December 1995, 565-580. Fong also cites W. Rader, *The Church and Racial Hostility: A History of Interpretation of Ephesians 2:11-22* (Tubingen: J.C. B. Mohr [Paul Siebeck]).

[17] J. Dunn, *Letter to the Romans* in G. Hawthorne, R. Martin, D. Reid, eds., *Dictionary of Paul and His Letters*, (Downers Grove: IVP, 1993) 839. Dunn continues, "This alone is sufficient to explain some of the characteristic elements and the message of the letter [to the Romans]: for example, 'who/what is a Jew?' (Rom 2:25-29); who are 'the elect of God'? (Rom 1:7; 8:33; 9:6-13; 11:5-7, 28-32); and the climactic position of Romans 9-11 and Romans 15:8-12."

The Judaizer Threat

7. Paul's letter to the Romans may have been written partly to pre-empt the Judaizing heresy that had plagued Paul's past. Paul mentioned those who slandered him (Ro. 3:8) and those who "cause divisions and put obstacles in your way" (Ro. 16:17)—earmarks of the Judaizers. But most importantly, Paul's letter to the Romans seeks to level the relationship of Jews and Gentiles in Christ and reconcile the two factions—thus *preventing* a hostile environment ripe for the heresy of the Judaizers.

8. Let's look at a few chapters in Romans that show how Paul dealt with the problem: Ro. 2:17-3:31 (equal basis theology); Ro. 14 (the "weak and the strong;" note verses 13 and 20—we should not hinder the spread of the gospel). F. F. Bruce defines the "weak" as "those who scrupulously abstained from certain kinds of food and paid religious respect to certain holy days, while the 'strong' (like Paul himself) had a more robust conscience with regard to such externalities." Paul admonishes neither group to impose its conscience on the other (the Jews with their limitations, the Gentiles with their liberty).

Teaching Idea

Do a class exercise. Read through Romans and identify the possible arguments of the Jews that Paul countered. For instance, we may conclude from Romans 2:12-24 that the Gentiles were boasting that they were custodians of the Law, and not like "Gentile sinners" (cf. Gal. 2:15). Romans 3:31 may indicate that the Jews accused Paul of nullifying the law. Record your observations.

3

Paul at a Crossroads

1. HAVE YOU EVER BEEN AT A CROSSROADS? Have you ever had to make a hard choice between what you would rather do and what you are obligated to do? This is precisely what Paul faced at Corinth. He had completed ten years of apostolic work, pioneering new churches "from Jerusalem all the way around to Illyricum" (Ro. 15:19), but now his work was finished in the regions of Galatia, Macedonia, and Achaia (Ro. 15:23).

2. We know that Paul desired to visit Rome in preparation for future apostolic endeavors into Spain (Ro. 1:10-13; 15:23-28; Acts 19:21) and he designed this letter to pave the way for his future ministry. However, Paul felt obligated to first complete the task of taking the contributions of the Gentile churches to Jerusalem. Paul wrote, "Now, however, I am on my way to Jerusalem in the service of the saints there. For Macedonia and Achaia were pleased to make a contribution for the poor among the saints in Jerusalem...So after I have completed this task and have made sure that they have received this fruit, I will go to Spain and visit you on the way" (Ro. 15:25-26, 28).

3. This delay meant that the gospel—particularly Paul's gospel emphasis[18] of righteousness apart from law and the inclusion of the Gentiles on an equal basis with the Jews—would not arrive at Rome in full detail for some time. Since Paul's presentation of this gospel to the Corinthians and Galatians only a couple of years before was met with misunderstanding and stubborn resistance,[19] especially from the Judaizers,[20] Paul probably felt the urgency to send a letter before he began his journey.

Mark Reasoner commented further:

> "Paul's gospel of a righteousness apart from Torah (3.21; 9.31; 10.4)...has clearly been construed as shamefully libertarian (6.1, 14-15), and Paul seeks to dissipate this notoriety."[21]

4. The Judaizers had found and opposed Paul time after time—would they not do so again at Rome?[22] If the gospel of the Judaizers (that righteousness is obtained by observing the law) had not already preceded Paul to Rome, it would

---

[18] τὸ εὐγγέλιόν μου– "my gospel" (Ro. 2:16; 16:25-26; cf. Gal. 1:11-12; 2:1-2; Eph. 3:6).

[19] See 1 Cor. 1:18-2:5 and the whole of Galatians, especially Gal. 1:6-3:14 and 6:11-16. In many ways, Romans is an expansion of the themes and Old Testament texts used in Galatians and 1 Corinthians.

[20] The name "Judaizers" is taken from Gal. 2:14 (ioudaizo). Paul had harsh words for the Judaizers (cf. Phil 3:2-4; Gal. 5:12). See the discussion in J. Becker, *The Faithfulness of God and the Priority of Israel in Paul's Letter to the Romans* in *The Romans Debate*, in Karl Donfried, editor, *The Romans Debate* Revised and Expanded Edition (Peabody, Massachusetts: 1991) 328.

[21] Mark Reasoner, *The Strong and the Weak: Romans 14:1-15:13 in Context* (Cambridge University Press, 1999) 224.

[22] Paul's greatest nemeses to reconciling Jewish Christians and Gentile Christians were the Judaizers. This group required circumcision and obedience to ceremonial law as conditions for membership in the community of believers. (The resultant separation of Jewish Christians from Gentile Christians at Galatia (Gal. 2:14-21) was probably not an isolated incident.) Paul mentioned those who slandered him (Ro. 3:8) and those who "cause divisions and put obstacles in your way" (Ro. 16:17)—earmarks of the Judaizers (Gal. 2:11-21). Paul encountered the Judaizers in Acts 15:5, 23; Gal. 2:3-5 and probably referred to them in Phil. 3:24.

eventually get there (cf. Ro. 16:17-18).[23] Thomas Schreiner wrote:

> He knew that doubts and questions had surfaced in the Roman congregations about his gospel, but he did not yet face full-fledged opponents. These apprehensions about Paul's teaching in Rome could be alleviated if his gospel were thoroughly explained, particularly on issues relating to Jews and Gentiles.[24]

5. In short, Paul stood at a crossroads. He had completed his apostolic work in Asia Minor and desired to introduce the gospel to the people of Spain. He was concerned both about his opponents and about the acceptance of the collection from the Gentile Christians of Asia Minor to their fellow Jewish believers in Jerusalem (Ro. 15:30-32). Since he could not continue on to Rome immediately, Paul fired off the letter we know as Romans before turning his attention to Jerusalem.

6. Paul wrote his epistle to the Romans to head off potential problems between Jewish Christians and Gentile Christians at Rome—the "same troubles he has been facing in Asia and Greece."[25] He did this primarily by writing a comprehensive explanation of the gospel and its effects on the relationship between Jews and Gentiles. Paul's missionary plans would be hindered (and perhaps thwarted) if the differences were not settled. If this thesis is correct, Paul's epistle to the Romans is preemptive and reconciling in its overall purpose.[26]

---

[23] Perhaps the Jewish Christians returning to Rome several years after the expulsion of Claudius may have brought it with them.
[24] Thomas Schreiner, *Romans* (Grand Rapids: Baker Book House, 1998) 21. All Rome would know that Paul was "not ashamed" of the gospel!
[25] Michael Goulder, *The Pauline Epistles* in Robert Alter and Frank Kermode, *The Literary Guide to the Bible*, (Cambridge: Harvard University Press, 1987) 497. T. W. Manson, *St. Paul's Letter to the Romans*, in *The Romans Debate*, 4, wrote: "Romans is the calm and collected summing-up of Paul's position as it had been hammered out in the heat of controversy during the previous months."
[26] I believe the epistle was thoroughly occasional. Romans was also directed to enlist the prayer support of the Christians at Rome (Ro. 15:30-32). There are several interrelated purposes for the letter. Reasoner (p. 236) gathers the themes

Teaching Ideas

Create a PowerPoint presentation called the "Background Situation of Romans." Use this for review. This could include maps of Paul's journeys and pictures of Emperor Claudius and the city of Corinth, as well as the overview points in Appendix B.

---

together under one theme or "topos:" "Paul, his gospel, and those who follow his gospel are not shameful."

4

The Greater Purpose of Reconciliation

1. FROM THE FOREGOING EXAMPLES we begin to see how each of the various topics in Paul's epistle fit within the greater purpose of reconciling Jewish Christians and Gentile Christians together. Paul made his theology subservient to the immediate situation at Rome. Remember that Paul needed a solid base of operations at Rome in order to prepare for his future mission endeavors into Spain. Further, Paul hopes that getting the attention of both groups directed toward missions into Spain will unite them in mutual effort. His missions designs are themselves reconciling.

2. He wrote extensively about the gospel to prevent the Judaizers from spoiling this opportunity. If the two factions *could not worship together*, the situation would be ripe for their heresy.

3. We know that Paul addressed the groups separately. At times he appears to address the Gentiles, and other times he seems to be in debate with the synagogue. Paul turned to one then the other to correct their boasting, high-minded, or judgmental attitudes (to the Jewish Christians: Ro. 2:1, 12, 17-18; 3:9, cf. Ro. 3:27; 4:2; to the Gentile Christians: Ro. 11:13, 17, 19-20, cf. Ro. 11:18; in general: Ro. 8:1; 12:3, 9; 13:13; 14:1-4, 13-17; 16:17).[27] In fact, Paul's whole teaching on justification by

---

[27] The word "krino" (to judge) and its forms occur ten times in the second chapter and then reappear in chapter fourteen. See Minear, 46. Minear quotes C.

faith is designed to bolster his point that we all come to Christ on an equal basis.[28] Neither group has a right to boast!

4. Paul often seems to place himself between two quarreling groups. At one moment he is exhorting the Gentiles as sinners; the next moment he is pointing his finger at the Jews for being judgmental: "You, therefore, have no excuse, you who pass judgment on someone else"[29] (Ro. 2:1), "Now you, if you call yourself a Jew; if you rely on the law and brag..." (Ro. 2:17). To one party he turned and declared, "All who sin apart from the law will also perish apart from the law..." (Ro. 2:12). Then he turned to the other party and said, "and all who sin under the law will be judged by the law." Lest the opponents turn on him, Paul identifies with them both and includes himself as a Jew: "What shall we conclude then? Are we any better?" (Ro. 3:9). One can almost imagine Paul with his hands extended in reconciliation to both groups.

Paul often anticipated the questions from the two sides and answered them thoroughly. (This ancient rhetorical form is called a "diatribe,"[30] or an extended dialogue with imaginary

---

K. Barrett regarding the significance of the sin of judgmentalism: "Behind all the sins of 1.29ff. lies the sin of idolatry which reveals man's ambition to put himself in the place of God and so to be his own Lord. But this is precisely what the judge does." C. K. Barrett, Epistle to the Romans (New York, 1957) 43.

[28] Here is where some make a case for the theme of Romans based on the frequency of the theological argument. Some see the theme of Romans as "righteousness by faith." The words righteous, righteousness, unrighteous, justice, justification, and so on, appear in the book of Romans sixty-five times. (See Ro 1:17, 32; 2:5, 13, 26; 3:5, 10, 20-22, 25-26; 4:3, 5-6, 9, 11, 13, 22, 24; 5:7, 17-19, 21; 6:13, 16, 18-20; 7:12; 8:4, 10; 9:28, 30-31; 10:3-6, 10.) However, the theological argument is subservient to the practical needs of the Jew/Gentile relationship. The points are: 1) Jews cannot be proud of works-righteousness in the Lord, and 2) faith-righteousness is possessed equally by Jew and Gentile. See also section "2.2 Evidence from Romans" in P. W. Barnet, *Opponents of Paul* in G. Hawthorne, R. Martin, D. Reid, eds., *Dictionary of Paul and His Letters*, 646.

[29] "You" has special emphasis in the Greek and it points a strong finger at the judgmental spirit of the Jews.

[30] See D. F. Watson, *Diatribe*, in G. Hawthorne, R. Martin, and D. Reid, editors, *Dictionary of Paul and His Letters* (Downers Grove: InterVarsity Press, 1993) 213-214.

participants [interlocutors] to persuade them.) His purpose was to bring the two factions to agreement and reconciliation through his persuasive arguments. Paul takes the Jewish Christian and Gentile Christian at Rome by the hand and makes them shake on it. Can we do any less?

5. When we gather the practical exhortations that Paul gives to the Romans we notice immediately a deliberate design by Paul to strengthen the relationships between Jewish Christians and Gentile Christians:[31]

   a. Ro. 2:1; 14:1-4, 13-17 – do not judge one another.
   b. Ro. 2:21 – do not be hypocritical.
   c. Ro. 3:9 – don't think that you are any better.
   d. Ro. 3:27; 4:2; 11:13, 17-18 – do not boast over others.
   e. Ro. 11:20 – do not be arrogant, but be afraid.
   f. Ro. 12:3 – do not be high-minded.
   g. Ro. 12:5 – each member belongs to all the others.
   h. Ro. 12:9 – honor one another above yourselves.
   i. Ro. 13:9 – love your neighbor as yourself.
   j. Ro. 13:13 – behave decently…not in dissension and jealousy.
   k. Ro. 14:1; 15:1-9 – accept the weak and do not please yourself.
   l. Ro. 14:9 – do not judge your brother.
   m. Ro. 14:13 – stop passing judgment on one another.
   n. Ro. 14:13-23 – do not put a stumbling block in front of your brother.
   o. Ro. 14:19 – do what leads to peace and mutual edification.

---

[31] Paul also includes practical countermeasures to the social problems at Rome (cf. Ro. 12:13, 16).

p. Ro. 16:17 – watch out for those who cause divisions and put obstacles in your way.

Whereas these exhortations may appear as random admonishments in the epistle, especially in the paraenetical section, taken together in view of the situation at Rome they become direct countermeasures linking the pieces of the epistle to the reconciliation problem at Rome.

Paul's strong admonition against passing judgment on someone else at Ro. 2:1 comes at the end of his lengthy discussion pertaining to the wrath of God "being revealed from heaven against all godlessness" (Ro. 1:18ff). A Jew might nod in agreement that the foregoing condemnation extended to Gentiles (certainly not us!), but would have been shocked out of his complacency by the finger pointed at him (Ro. 2:1). Thus, Paul's whole opening argument seeks to level the ground between the two groups.

Teaching Ideas

Do a class exercise. Find the axioms in Romans 14:1-15:13 upon which Paul seeks to build unity.[32] Record your observations.

---

[32] I am indebted for this idea to Paul Minear, pp. 17-20. See handout, "Paul's Axioms of Romans 14:1-15:13."

6. But Paul is not at all finished. If the Jews "brag about [their] relationship to God" (Ro. 2:17) and "brag about the Law" (Ro. 2:23), yet do the same things as the Gentiles, are they not equal lawbreakers? God is not unjust in bringing His wrath on Jews as well (Ro. 3:5). Jews are not "any better" for "Jews and Gentiles alike are all under sin" (Ro. 3:9; cf. 3:22-23; 5:12, 18). Every "mouth may be silenced" (Ro. 3:19). Boasting is "excluded" (Ro. 3:27).

   Even Abraham had nothing to boast about (Ro. 4:2) since his righteousness was by faith! Paul's lengthy argument about Abraham and justification by faith in chapter four is not just a theological argument; Paul still levels the ground between the two groups and silences any Jewish pride.

   Ultimately, none can boast, for "from Him and through Him, and to Him are all things" (Ro. 11:36). No one has any ground to be prideful! Pride has no place in Christ!

7. Let's view another example from Romans 13 that shows how the situation may have prompted Paul's exhortations. In a very real sense, the Jews suffered a form of "ethnic cleansing" at the hands of the Roman authorities. There would have been associated business loss, perhaps even confiscation of property. When the Jews (and Jewish Christians) returned, it is reasonable to assume that there would be a natural reluctance on their part to treat the authorities with "respect" and "honor." Those who had suffered financially may have also expressed a reluctance to pay "taxes" or "revenue" (Ro. 13:1-7). Paul's words make perfect sense in this context.

8. Before we pass from this subject, we need to remember that Paul's calling included reconciliation. As a Jew by birth and called to be an apostle to Gentiles, Paul represented *a unique bridge between the two races.* Marvin Wilson wrote:

   > A Diaspora Jew from Tarsus, Paul was uniquely equipped for this gentile mission. He was knowledgeable in the rich legacy of his people through his Pharisaic training under the famous Jewish teacher Gamaliel. But being a Roman

citizen (Acts 22:25-29) from a Mediterranean seaport, he was also thoroughly acquainted with the prevailing customs of the Greco-Roman world.[33]

9. Paul also made every effort to demonstrate the unity that should exist between Jews and Gentiles. "The massive effort that he put into the collection for the poor of Jerusalem and his willingness to die in the process of delivering it indicate the importance he placed on the unity of Jew and Gentile in one church."[34] The offering not only provided financial relief to the needy Jewish believers at Jerusalem, but made a major statement of racial reconciliation as well.

10. Paul labored under "great heaviness and continual sorrow" (Ro. 9:5) for his kinsmen, the Jews. Although his missions work remained foremost in his mind, the reconciliation of Jewish and Gentile Christians was not merely pragmatic, but issued from deep sensitivity and concern.

---

[33] Marvin Wilson, *Our Father Abraham: Jewish Roots of the Christian Faith*, (Grand Rapids: Eerdmans, 1989) 46.

[34] D. Madvig, *The Missionary Preaching of Paul: A Problem in New Testament Theology,* **Journal of the Evangelical Theological Society**, vol. 20, no. 2, 1977, 151.

5

Equal Basis Theology

1. WE HAVE SEEN HOW THE BACKGROUND of the epistle helps explain each of its various theological and practical parts. The major theological point that Paul establishes in the first three chapters is what we termed "equal basis theology." This doctrine states that we all come to Christ the same way—by faith, whether Jew or Gentile. Hence, we have no basis for boasting because of our works, heritage, or race. (See Galatians 6:13.)

2. Throughout these chapters, Paul makes several theological arguments for the equal basis of all humanity. These are summarized below:

    a. **God has revealed Himself to all humanity through creation** (called "general revelation"), therefore everyone should recognize Him and everyone is without excuse (Ro. 1:18-20). "The intricate design of every aspect of this universe shows the intelligence of the one who brought it into existence."[35]

    b. **All humanity has rejected God and rebelled against Him** (called "original sin," Ro. 1:19-32; 3:9-20). Everyone is guilty before God and without excuse (Ro.

---

[35] E. C. James, *Romans: Amazing Grace* (Meridian Publications, 1991) 30. The interdependency of the intricate details discounts evolution. The similarities among the species and the irreducible complexity of all creatures speak of a Master designer.

2:1).[36] Paul exposed the general depravity[37] of man, especially the idolatry of the Gentiles (Ro. 1:18-22), then showed the same sinfulness among Jews (2:1-29). Sin is universal.

Paul quoted several Psalms and Isaiah to show the utter depravity of man. Man's *throat* is an "open grave," his *tongue* practices "deceit," his *lips* have the "poison of vipers," his *mouth* is "full of cursing and bitterness," his *feet* are "swift to shed blood," and his *eyes* have "no fear of God" (Ro. 3:13-18). In short, the whole person—his entire being—is adversely affected by sin. And just in case Jewish Christians thought that this addressed Gentiles only, Paul reminded them that the law was written for those "who are under the law" (Ro. 3:19).[38]

c. **Everyone will be judged and rewarded on an equal basis before God** for what they have done (Ro. 2:6-10, 25-29). The Jews cannot rationalize their exemption from judgment by condemning Gentiles. We are all subject to His wrath because we are all sinners. Our works reveal what we are. Leon Morris comments:

They [works] are the outward expression of what the person is deep down. In the believer they are the expression of faith, in the unbeliever the expression of unbelief...The Jew cannot rest in a fancied security of

---

[36] Paul later declares that all creation is subjected to "futility" (Ro. 8:20).

[37] By depravity we do not mean that man is as bad as he will ever be. Nor do we mean that man sins all the time. Depravity means that the sin nature has been inherited by all humanity from Adam and that we all therefore have a preponderant tendency to sin (Ro. 3:23; 5:12-15, 21).

[38] Sin has three basic characteristics: it grows, it spreads, and it kills. Gruenler notes, "Yet so willful is the rebellious human heart that it is not content to sin in isolation but demands the right to carry others down in corporate sin." Walter Elwell, *Evangelical Commentary on the Bible* (Grand Rapids: Baker Book House, 1989) 931.

privilege but must look to the day when his works will be subjected to the divine scrutiny.[39]

On the day of judgment, every mouth will be stopped and "the whole world held accountable to God" (Ro. 3:19).

d. **God is just and true, He does not show favoritism** (Ro. 2:2, 11; 3:4, 26). He is impartial. The Jews cannot count on their privileged position and responsibility as recipients of the Law and the prophet's utterances to justify themselves.

e. **All are justified by faith in the atonement of Christ** (Ro. 3:22-25, 28). We all come to Christ the same way.

If we were equally guilty before, we all may equally receive the grace of God and be justified by faith now. This is the power of salvation. The gospel can rescue the sinner completely from the snare of sin and death. Here we find that boasting is excluded (Ro. 3:27), for salvation is by grace. It is neither earned nor deserved (Ro. 11:6).

f. **God is the God of everyone** (Ro. 3:29-30). God is not the exclusive God of any one people.[40] The Gentiles had many gods, including national gods. However, since there is but one God, He is the God of all nations. (See Isaiah 45:22.)

We could summarize these arguments as follows: Since God has revealed Himself to everyone, everyone can be judged guilty in an equitable way. Since God is the just Judge of all humanity, He will receive all who have faith in the atonement of Jesus Christ and He will condemn all those who do not have faith. God will not show favoritism to anyone; He will judge everyone on an equal basis.

---

[39] Leon Morris, *The Epistle to the Romans* (Grand Rapids: Wm. B. Eerdmans Pub. Co., 1988) 116.
[40] Op. Cit. 187-188.

3. Paul bolsters this equal basis theology by his repeated emphasis on "all" or "everyone" coming to Christ on the same terms.[41] Paul argued his equal basis theology in Romans 3-5 by using all-inclusive language. By the end of chapter 5 the leveling effect of the gospel does not leave the reader doubt about the equality of those who are in Christ:

   a. Ro. 3:9 – all are under sin.
   b. Ro. 3:19 – God holds everyone accountable.
   c. Ro. 3:20 – observing the law makes no one righteous in his sight.
   d. Ro. 3:22 – righteousness imputed to all who believe.
   e. Ro. 3:29 – only one God exists for Jews and Gentiles.[42]
   f. Ro. 4:16 –Abraham's offspring—both those of the law and those of faith—inherit the promise of salvation.
   g. Ro. 4:16 – Abraham is the father of us all.
   h. Ro. 5:12 – death came to all men, because all sinned.
   i. Ro. 5:18 – since one trespass condemned all men, so also one act of righteousness justified and brought life for all men.

---

[41] See Reasoner, 229; A. Wedderburn, *The Purpose and Occasion of Romans Again*, in *The Romans Debate*, 195. G. Bronkamm, *Last Will and Testament*, in *The Romans Debate*, 25, wrote: "It is not by chance that the words 'all,' 'each,' or the negative 'no one' are used in no other letter of Paul as often as in Romans."

[42] Paul states this explicitly in Acts 17:26-28.

Paul declared that all those who are in Christ (Ro. 8:1) have received the "Spirit of sonship" (Ro. 8:15) and were "heirs...and coheirs" (Ro. 8:17) with Christ. This foreshadowed what Paul would say about the inclusion of the Gentiles in Eph. 2:11-14, where those in Christ were no longer "separate from Christ, excluded from citizenship in Israel and foreigners to the covenants of the promise." Jews and Gentiles were reconciled together into one new creation.

From Romans 8:18 to 11:36 Paul again made several points showing the equal basis of Jews and Gentiles:

a. Ro. 8:32 – God gives Christ for us all; Christ gives inheritance for all in Him.

b. Ro. 8:28-30 – we are all brothers and sisters in the divine plan.

c. Ro. 9:6-9 – true Israel consists of all those who receive the promise by faith.

d. Ro. 9:12, 16 – election is by God's purpose, not man's works.

e. Ro. 9:23-24 – God prepares both Jews and Gentiles "in advance for His glory."

f. Ro. 10:4 – God extends righteousness to everyone who believes.

g. Ro. 10:11-13, 18 – God's invites all.

h. Ro. 9:13, 27-30; 10:16-17 – many rejected God's invitation.

i. Ro. 11:17-24 – Jew and Gentile can take part of the Olive Tree.

j. Ro. 11:32 – everyone is disobedient; everyone may receive mercy.

Paul summarized his equal basis argument:[43]

> For there is no difference between Jew and Gentile—the same Lord is Lord of all and richly blesses all who call on him, for, "Everyone who calls on the name of the Lord will be saved." —Ro. 10:12-13

> For God has bound all men over to disobedience so that he may have mercy on them all.—Ro. 11:32

F. F. Bruce noted:

> What is emphasized above all, however, is God's good will towards all men, Jews and Gentiles alike. If, at an earlier stage of his argument, Paul has concluded that "there is no distinction, since all have sinned" and stand alike in need of God's grace, now he concludes that "there is no distinction between Jew and Greek,…for God has consigned all to disobedience, that he may have mercy upon all" (Romans 10:12; 11:32).[44]

Despite the outward differences, the nature of every human derives from the same lump of fallen clay. Only those in Christ are fit for the Potter's hands.

---

[43] Reasoner (p. 229) noted "the way in which Paul uses 'all' or comparable expressions to advance this purpose of promoting ethnic equality. Indeed it is worth observing that major sections of Romans end with these inclusive pronouncements of God's mercy to all (11.32, 36; 15:8-12)."

[44] F. F. Bruce, *Paul: Apostle of the Heart Set Free*, 336.

4. Paul also brings in a concept that would have shocked the Judaizers:

> It was not through law that Abraham and his offspring received the promise that he would be heir of the world, but through the righteousness that comes by faith. For if those who live by law are heirs, faith has no value and the promise is worthless, because law brings wrath.—Ro. 4:13-15a

Paul shows us, contrary to the view of the Judaizers, that we are no longer under the law. In fact, because Christ died for us, we are dead to the law (not just to sin):

> So, my brothers, you also died to the law through the body of Christ, that you might belong to another, to him who was raised from the dead, in order that we might bear fruit to God.—Ro. 7:4

> Therefore, there is now no condemnation for those who are in Christ Jesus, because through Christ Jesus the law of the Spirit of life set me free from the law of sin and death.—Ro. 8:1-2

Paul's important final conclusion returns us to the equal basis theology that he established at the beginning of his epistle:

> Christ is the end of the law so that there may be righteousness for everyone who believes.—Ro. 10:4

Paul does not say that we are socially antinomian, a charge that must have been leveled by his opponents, but rather that we now have righteousness by faith. (This new way enables us to keep the righteous requirements of the law through the Spirit, not through the old way of the letter.) Consequently, we come to Christ on an equal basis—we are on the same footing before God no matter who we are.

5. Many expositors have looked at this last verse (and Romans as a whole) and emphasized the law, righteousness, or faith. We must not view each theological piece separately, but realize that Paul unites all these into one theme for the practical purpose of bringing the two groups together. Jacob Jervell noted, "We have every reason to stress that justification by faith apart from law is not the theme of Romans. That theme was treated in Galatians. The theme of Romans is this: the righteousness of God is revealed through faith apart from law, first for the Jews, then to the Greeks, and at the end to all Israel."[45]

6. Having created a level playing field for all people, and specifically between Jews and Gentiles, Paul leaves no theological reason for the two factions to worship separately. Now he is able to bring the two groups together.

---

[45] Jacob Jervell, *The Letter to Jerusalem*, in *The Romans Debate*, 59. I would only add that Paul further develops his previous letter to the Galatians and applies it specifically to the needs of the Romans.

6

Reconciliation of Jews and Gentiles in the Broader Context of the New Testament

1. WHEN PUTTING A THOUSAND-PIECE PUZZLE TOGETHER, what is the first thing you do after pouring the pieces out on the table and turning them right side up? Don't you find all the edge pieces and begin putting the puzzle frame together? Well, we've been piecing together the background and purpose of Paul's epistle to the Romans, but it would be helpful to take a moment and put what we've discovered into the larger framework of the New Testament. This framework helps us see the complete picture, and to make sure what we have assembled so far fits correctly into the puzzle as a whole.

2. In other words, if what we have been saying about Romans is true, we should find Paul's other epistles confirming our thesis. If the problem of Jew/Gentile relationships is the critical issue Paul addresses in his epistle to the Romans, it would also make sense that it is addressed elsewhere—at least in his letters to cities where both Jewish Christians and Gentile Christians reside. In fact, we shall see that Romans is not a "one off" epistle. That is, the issues centering on the unity between the two groups are not isolated to Roman Christianity, but, instead, Paul tackles these at other times and other places. Without appearing to exaggerate one issue above other important ones,

getting these two groups to accept one another and worship together (Ro. 15:7) was one of the most difficult problems facing Paul—and the Church—during its fledgling years.

3. Appendix G delves into the racial setting in the New Testament and the New Testament world, but I want to here focus on Acts, Galatians, and Ephesians which are only covered briefly there and how Luke and Paul address the inclusion of the Gentiles into God's people. To these books we now turn.

4. Acts was written by Luke, a close traveling companion of Paul, and an eyewitness of many events recorded in this book. Roughly the latter half of the book recounts Paul's apostolic efforts during three journeys in and around Asia Minor and the Grecian peninsula, and Paul's final visit to Jerusalem. Acts not only traces the movement of Christianity out from its birthplace in Judea to the Mediterranean world, but also *the parallel/progressive movement of Christianity out from its Jewish roots into the Gentile world.* In fact, Luke seems to deliberately record the events that argue for the inclusion of the Gentiles into God's plan. The following is a quick overview emphasizing this point.

5. The gospel was preached to the Samaritans in Acts 8:4-25. Although the Samaritans were not Jews, they weren't exactly Gentiles either. This was only a half-step out from Judaism. But it was significant enough for the apostles to send Peter and John to check it out. We should note that the Holy Spirit was given by the laying on of hands—definitely confirming that the Samaritans had become believers. We cannot emphasize this enough. It was the presence of the Spirit that confirmed to everyone the fact that the Samaritans had believed. Without this supernatural experience providing definite confirmation, there would have been reason for the apostles to question that those outside Judaism had—or could—become the people of God.

6. By itself, the fact that the Samaritans had received the gift of the Spirit was not so significant or challenging to the view that

salvation was for the Jews alone. But the expansion of Christ's kingdom didn't stop there. Next we find Philip preaching to and baptizing an Ethiopian, probably a proselyte (cf. vs. 27), but nevertheless a Gentile! Samaritans? Gentile proselytes? What is this coming to?

7. There immediately follows the important passage of Paul's Damascus road conversion and his direct call from Christ to go to the Gentiles (Acts 9:9-13). Christ declared, "This man is my chosen instrument to carry my name before the Gentiles and their kings and before the people of Israel" (vs. 15). By this commission, Christ had clearly broken down the walls between Jews and Gentiles and declared His (continued) intentions to reach all nations (cf. Mt. 28:19-20).

8. We are interrupted in tracing out the missionary work of Paul to see the "God-fearer" Cornelius and his household converted in Acts 10 through Peter's preaching. In this whole episode, Luke records how Peter sees a vision from heaven demonstrating to him that he "should not call any man impure or unclean" (vs. 28)—meaning Gentiles. While Peter explained the gospel to Cornelius and his household, "the Holy Spirit came on all who heard the message. The circumcised believers who had come with Peter were astonished that the gift of the Holy Spirit had been poured out even on the Gentiles" (vs. 44). The astonishment of the Jews derived not from the fact that God pours out His Spirit, but from the fact that these Gentiles were uncircumcised. Up until this point, circumcision marked off the people of God. Now the Spirit had marked these Gentiles as God's people without circumcision. The Holy Spirit had again confirmed—with profound definiteness—that Gentiles were included as God's people.

9. Preaching to the Gentiles immediately brings criticism down on Peter from the Jews who had not witnessed the outpouring on Cornelius' household (Acts 11). Peter explains that the Holy Spirit "came on them as he had come on us at the beginning" (vs. 15, referring to the outpouring at Pentecost in Acts 2).

There was no disputing the fact that the Spirit had fallen on the Gentiles without requiring them to first become Jews. For the moment the debate was put to rest, but Jewish scruples and racial prejudice are hard to eradicate. The issue would appear again at the Jerusalem gathering in Acts 15.

10. Not long after this Paul is ordained and commissioned, along with Barnabas, to minister to the Gentiles (Acts 13:1ff; cf. 26:15-18) and they begin their first apostolic journey. Their evangelistic work, though often finding opportunity to begin at the local synagogues, soon faced rejection by the Jews:

> Then Paul and Barnabas answered them boldly: "We had to speak the word of God to you [Jews] first. Since you reject it and do not consider yourselves worthy of eternal life, we now turn to the Gentiles. For this is what the Lord has commanded us: "'I have made you a light for the Gentiles, that you may bring salvation to the ends of the earth.'"

Paul echoes this same sentiment later in Acts 18:6.

11. We have already examined Acts 15 (see chapter 2; cf. Appendix G) and its implications for the Jew/Gentile setting and we will not discuss it in detail here, except to observe how this fits within Luke's continued narrative recounting the difficulties surrounding the inclusion of the Gentiles in the people of God. This event constitutes a significant turning point for the whole issue. The result is that the apostles accommodate the scruples of the Jews while removing the barrier of circumcision for the Gentiles.

12. Let me re-emphasize a note above. Luke shows that the reception of the Spirit by the Gentiles was something definite—demonstrated by clear supernatural evidence. In other words, if Paul had been asked by the Jewish Christians or Judaizers, "How do we know that the Gentiles have really been brought in as the people of God without the requirement of circumcision (and I'm sure some such question was raised), Paul would have responded that there were definite signs that they had received the Holy Spirit—speaking in tongues,

prophesying, etc. They all understood that the reception of the Spirit would not have been possible unless they were accepted as the people of God. In contrast, to simply say that the Gentiles had the Spirit because they had confessed faith, or had the "tingles" or even were baptized would not do. That would not have convinced the Jewish Christians. However, a definite, supernatural sign provided the assurance necessary to convince everyone.

13. Paul's second apostolic journey follows shortly after this gathering (Acts 15:36ff). The decision of the apostles must have bolstered the confidence of Paul and his companions in their ministry to the Gentiles. Paul's journeys would take him clear around to Illyricum and back (Ro. 15:19), usually reaching out to Jews first, then Gentiles. But in the final analysis, Paul "shook out his clothes in protest" (Acts 18:6) to the Jews for their refusal to receive the gospel, and turned instead to the Gentiles (Acts 28:28).

14. Galatians correlates with Romans in several ways and much of this contains subject matter related to the Jew/Gentile issue. This is summarized below:

Galatians	Romans
2:6 – God does not judge externally (show favoritism)	Ro. 2:11
2:7-9 – Paul Preached to Gentiles as Peter to the Jews	Ro. 15:16
2:15 – Not justified by works of the Law, but by faith	Ro. 3-4 (3:26)
2:17 – Does Christ promote sin? Absolutely not!	Ro. 6:1, 15
3:3; 5.16 – A work of the Spirit/Live by the Spirit	Ro. 8
3:6-9, 14-18 – Precedent of Abraham's Faith (Ge. 15:6)	Ro. 4
3:8 – all nations blessed through Abraham/father of many nations	Ro. 4:17-18
3:11 – "Righteous shall live by faith" (Hab. 2:4).	Ro. 1:17
3:19 – Purpose of the Law – "Is the Law opposed to the purposes of God? Absolutely not!" (vs. 21)	Ro. 7

(Continued on next page.)

Galatians	Romans
3:26-28 – All inclusive language used.	Ro. 3:22; 4:16, etc.
5:17 – Conflict of Flesh and Spirit	Ro. 7:15-23
6:13 – Not even those who are circumcised obey the Law."	Ro. 1-2 (2:25)
6:13 – Boasting about your flesh	Ro. 2:17
5:6; 6:15 – Neither circumcision nor uncircumcision means anything	Ro. 3

15. The bottom line is that neither circumcision nor uncircumcision guarantees our place in the family of God. Jews cannot depend on the Law, or their works—it is all a matter of faith in Christ Jesus.

16. But this must also be lived out in our relationships with one another. It is not enough to simply acknowledge our equal standing in Christ (Gal. 3:28), but we must also recognize that relationships within the community of faith are also forever changed. Paul illustrates this by recounting an incident in which he rebukes Peter for his hypocrisy in these matters. Peter had eaten with the Gentiles until members of the circumcision group joined them. Peter then separated himself from the Gentiles and even persuaded Barnabas to follow him. Paul's sharp rebuke of Peter's segregationist actions must have stung everyone's conscience:

> "You are a Jew, yet you live like a Gentile and not like a Jew. How is it, then, that you force Gentiles to follow Jewish customs? "We who are Jews by birth and not 'Gentile sinners' know that a man is not justified by observing the law, but by faith in Jesus Christ.

17. Philip Payne explains:

> The Judaizers demanded observance of special days, months, seasons, and years (Gal. 4:10). Paul regarded this as a return to the slavery of legalism and a denial of the heart of the gospel (4:8-11). These requirements had the practical

effect of elevating the Jews to a status with special privileges over the Gentiles, who were being treated as second-class citizens in the church. The entire book of Galatians is a frontal attack against favored status or privileges being granted to Jews over Gentiles.[46]

18. When we turn to Ephesians, we find one of the largest passages addressing the inclusion of the Gentiles in the people of God: Eph. 2:11-3:13. Paul characterizes the pre-redemptive relationship between Jews and Gentiles as having a "dividing wall of hostility" (2:14) between them. The Gentiles were "separate from Christ," "excluded from citizenship from Israel," "foreigners to the covenants" and "without hope" (2:12). But in Christ, the wall of separation was destroyed, the hostility was put to death, and one new person created from the two (2:15). This new person is neither Jew nor Gentile, but a new humanity. The Message Bible paraphrases, "Instead of continuing with two groups of people separated by centuries of animosity and suspicion, he created a new kind of human being, a fresh start for everybody."[47]

19. Being formed in Christ, this new person takes on His characteristics by the work of the Spirit. Neither obedience to commandments and regulations nor proper initiation into a new Jewish sect constitutes this new person, but grace through faith produced a new "workmanship," or even "masterwork" (2:8-9; cf. 2 Cor. 5:17) in Him. The racial tensions, animosity, prejudice, and segregation dissolve before the new humanity in Christ Jesus.

---

[46] Philip Payne, *Man and Woman, One in Christ: An Exegetical and Theological Study of Paul's Letters* (Grand Rapids: Zondervan, 2009) 82.

[47] Eugene H. Peterson, *The Message : The Bible in Contemporary Language* (Colorado Springs, Colo.: NavPress, 2002).

20. Several of Paul's other letters briefly take up the Jew/Gentile and other related issues. These are listed below.[48]

Topic	References
Inclusion of the Gentiles	Col. 1:24-29; 3:9-11; 1 Tim. 3:16
One God of Both Jews and Gentiles	1 Tim. 2:3-7
Disobedience of Israel	1 Cor. 1:23-24; 1 Thess. 2:14-16
Reconciliation of All Things	Col. 1:19-22

All of this shows that Paul considered reconciliation of Jews and Gentiles as critically important and addressed the issue accordingly in his epistles.

---

[48] I am indebted to James Ware, *Synopsis of the Pauline Letters in Greek in English* (Grand Rapids: Baker, 2010) for the topics and references cited. On a side note, all of this demonstrates a unity on a social-historical level among Paul's letters and with Acts.

7

Paul's Core Values

1. BEFORE WE INVESTIGATE THE HEART OF ROMANS (chapters 5-11), let us pause a moment and reflect on the practical issues culled from the background and purpose of the epistle. We've discussed them to some degree already, but let's present them as a list of Core Values that would have been important to Paul. In other words, what does the Book of Romans show us that Paul valued? (Answers are footnoted.)

   - Paul valued _____.
   Gaining new ground for the Kingdom of God was the motive that drove Paul constantly onward (see Acts 20:24). You sense that Paul would not be satisfied unless everyone became a Christian.

   - Paul valued _____.
   He knew the importance of Christ's justification and redemption and countenanced no substitute.

   - Paul valued _____.
   Although good theology is subservient to "practicology," good theology is the prerequisite to good "practicology." What we believe about God (theology) determines how we behave.

   - Paul valued _____.
   There is no room for prejudicial attitudes for Paul. The gospel has leveled the ground among us all.

- Paul valued _____.
  Separate communities of worship become kindling for prejudice, dissension, and misunderstanding. We also see not uniformity emphasized, but unity in diversity.

- Paul valued _____.
  He knew that without their generosity, prayers (Ro. 15:31), and logistical support, his missions work would be more difficult and less successful.

- Paul valued _____.
  The collection from the Christian Gentiles to the Christian Jews at Rome took precedence to his personal desires.[49]

2. Above all else, we see a deep passion and love for Christ and His Kingdom. Everything else seemed to Paul only a distraction.

3. How does each of these values impact our lives? Do we share the same values? Are these values important today? How should we work these apostolic values into the values of the local church?

---

[49] Answers are: apostolic work and missions; his gospel; good theology; racial reconciliation; worshipping together in unity; support from the local congregation, and fiscal responsibility.

8

Our Relationship to the Law

1. AS WE MENTIONED BEFORE, Paul sometimes addresses the Gentile Christians and sometimes the Jewish Christians in his epistle. He has very clearly leveled the ground between the two groups by his gospel and wants to reconcile them. In Romans 5 Paul addresses both groups with a very clear summary of the gospel, including justification by faith and Christ's blood (verses 1 and 9), and reconciliation to God (verses 10-11).

Paul then brings in the final argument to "nail the lid shut" on his equal basis theology in Romans 5:12-19. Here Paul compares the sin of Adam with the gift of Christ. He shows how Adam brought death to *all humankind* through his trespass, while Christ's death brought justification and life to *all humankind* (whether Jews or Gentiles):

> Consequently, just as the result of one trespass was condemnation for all men, so also the result of one act of righteousness was justification that brings life for all men. For just as through the disobedience of the one man the many were made sinners, so also through the obedience of the one man the many will be made righteous.—Ro. 5:18-19

Paul leaves the two groups with no room to argue. We all come to Christ the same way.

2. Paul next comments on the purpose of the law, something that would be foremost upon the minds of the Jewish Christians. In other words, the Jewish Christians would be the first to ask, "If we do come to Christ in the same manner as Gentiles, then why did God give us the law? What is its purpose?" Paul gives the answer in verses 20-21:

> The law was added so that the trespass might increase. But where sin increased, grace increased all the more, so that, just as sin reigned in death, so also grace might reign through righteousness to bring eternal life through Jesus Christ our Lord.—Ro. 5:20-21

3. Now this opens the door to a discussion with the Jewish Christians about a most important issue: *our relationship to the law*. When we look at the next series of chapters, Paul begins several sub-sections with questions that any reasonable Jewish Christian might raise, and probably did, considering the twenty years of Paul's preaching up to this point:

> "What shall we say, then? Shall we go on sinning so that grace may increase?"—Ro. 6:1

> "What then? Shall we sin because we are not under law but under grace?"—Ro. 6:15

> "What shall we say, then? Is the law sin?"—Ro. 7:7

> "Did that which is good (the Law), then, become death to me?"—Ro. 7:13

To these questions Paul responds decidedly, "By no means!" (Ro. 6:2, 15; 7:7, 13; [9:14; 11:1; 11:11]).[50]

In discussing this issue and answering these questions, Paul covers some of the most profound "practicology" ever written. For in these chapters (6-8) Paul reveals the struggle between our old and new natures and spells out how to live in the Spirit.

---

[50] μὴ γένοιτο. This seems to be a favorite Pauline response (see Galatians 2:17 and 3:21).

But the first and foremost principle we must take away from the text is that Paul addresses our relationship to the law. It is no longer our schoolmaster (to borrow a term from Galatians 3:24). We are no longer under its supervision. Now "we serve in the new way of the Spirit, and not in the old way of the written code" (Ro. 7:6). We are dead to the law and now live by the law of the Spirit of life in Christ Jesus (Ro. 8:1-4).

Being dead to the law does *not* mean that we no longer have to live holy lives. God's character is still reflected in the law—His holiness, righteousness, and goodness. The law is not something evil—the law is not the problem, we are! What has changed is our relationship to the law. We are no longer "to be under its condemnation or obligated to undertake the impossible task of fulfilling it on our own."[51] We have been set free to obey the righteous requirements of the law through the enablement of the Spirit, not through works of the flesh.

4. Paul wraps up this whole section with a final series of questions and answers (Ro. 8:31-39) that show the powerlessness of the law to point a finger of judgment against us!

5. We should take a moment to summarize Paul's explanation of the law throughout the epistle.

   Paul does not abandon or denounce the law, as some had charged unjustifiably. The law has several important functions:

   a. **It defines sin and awakens the conscience to sin** (Ro. 3:20). Paul put it this way: "where there is no law there is no transgression" (Ro. 4:15; 5:13b).

   b. **It declares everyone a sinner.** "The law was added so that the trespass might increase" (Ro. 5:20). Smedes notes, "The law pins the sinner down, nails him at every corner; it sweeps the whole of life into its net and brands every infraction a culpable act of rebellion

---

[51] Elwell, 938.

(Rom. 7:7-9)."[52] (See Deut. 31:24-26, where the law is "as a testimony against you!")

c. **It condemns those who disobey it** (Ro. 5:18). The law declares the penalty for each kind of sin. Paul said that it "brings wrath" (Ro. 4:15). "The written code kills, because it declares the will of God without imparting the power to do it, and pronounces the death-sentence on those who break it."[53]

d. **It actually intensifies the desire for sin.** It stirs up "the sense of sin of which humanity is aware" (Ro. 3:19-20; 7:7-25).[54] In some ways the law is designed to prevent sin, but because of the sin nature, the law actually multiplies it. F. F. Bruce comments:

> According to Paul, the law not only brings sin to light; it forbids sin, indeed, but it stimulates the very thing it forbids. In fact, says Paul, "the power of sin is the law" (1 Corinthians 15:56).[55]

e. **It exposes the lack of personal righteousness because of the weakness of the flesh** (Ro. 8:3). No one has been able to keep the standard required by the law.

Due to our sinful nature, we lack the power to keep the law (Ro. 8:3). The only way to overcome sin is to die to it (in Christ) and receive the life of the Spirit. The only way to fulfill the law is to die to it—thereby coming out from under its yoke of works/righteousness. Paul writes: we have "died to the law" (Ro. 7:4), we are "set free from the law of sin and death" (Ro. 8:2), and "Christ is the end of the law" (Ro. 10:4).

---

[52] L. Smedes, *Union With Christ* (Grand Rapids: Wm. B. Eerdmans Pub. Co., 1983) 71.
[53] Bruce, 200.
[54] Elwell, 936.
[55] Bruce, 194.

Teaching Ideas

Use Appendix C to create a white board or PowerPoint presentation called "Romans and the Law." Use this for review.

Use Appendix D to create a white board or PowerPoint presentation called "Moral Absolutes and Principles" to demonstrate Paul's principles/axioms in Romans.

9

The Core of Paul's Theology

1. IN ROMANS 6-8, WE ENCOUNTER THE CORE of Paul's theology. By "core" I don't mean a narrow or restricted theology, but an essential theology. What I mean is that Paul returned consistently to the Christ Event and its application to our lives when dealing with the problems in the fledgling churches. The death, burial, resurrection, and ascension of Christ—the Christ Event—provides the fulcrum upon which all his doctrine turns.

2. Paul's letter to the Romans is no exception. He brings the Christ Event to bear on the reconciliation needs at Rome by showing that: 1) both Jews and Gentiles come to Christ on an equal basis *through our death and resurrection in Him*, and 2) that our *unity in Christ* now opens a new way of life for us in the Spirit, no longer through the law.

3. In fact, to the Galatians (Gal. 2:11-21; 3:13, 26-29; 6:15-16), Ephesians (Eph. 2:13-16), and to the Romans as well (Ro. 3), Paul refers to the reconciling affects of the Christ Event on Jews and Gentiles, and belies the persistent, widespread problem between the two groups in first century Christianity.

4. To Paul, the gospel is not just "good news," it is the whole drama of the Christ Event from crucifixion to ascension—from the cross to the throne. Whether dealing with doctrine or practical application, Paul returned to the Christ Event for the answer. In the same way, it is imperative that we understand

each step of the Christ Event *and its significance* so that we can adjust our thinking and apply the truth to our lives. We will call this "mapping the Christ Event."

5. A graphical summary of the Christ Event is given below:

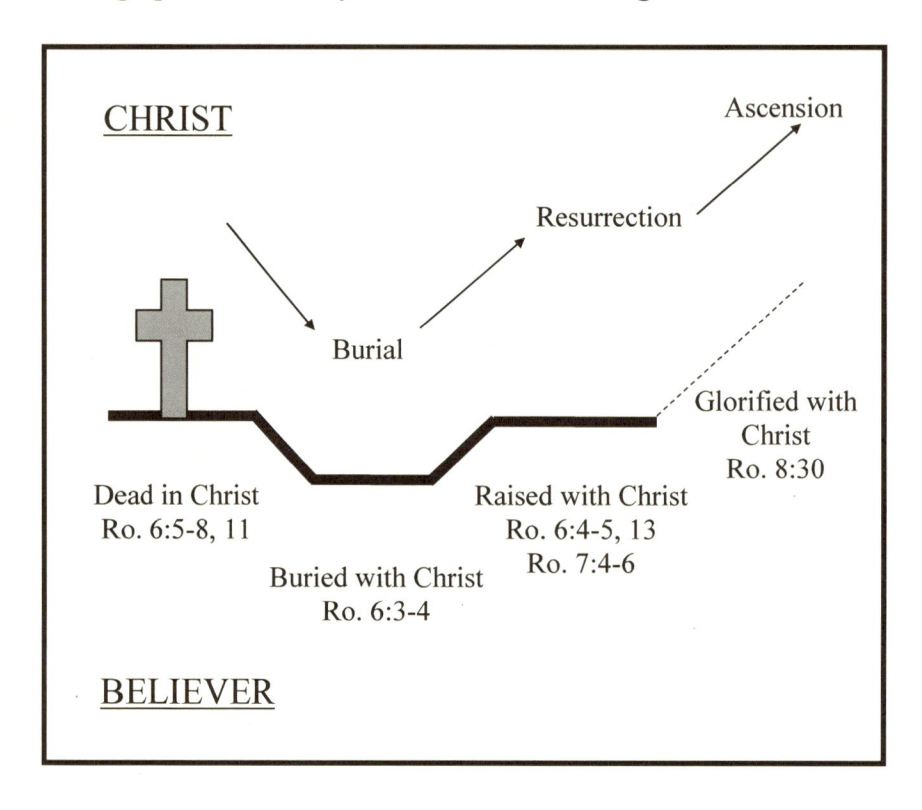

```
CHRIST                                    Ascension
                                         ↗
                            Resurrection ↗
                           ↗
                    ↘
                   Burial
    ✝                              ........ Glorified with
                                              Christ
                                              Ro. 8:30
Dead in Christ              Raised with Christ
Ro. 6:5-8, 11               Ro. 6:4-5, 13
                                Ro. 7:4-6
              Buried with Christ
              Ro. 6:3-4

BELIEVER
```

Teaching Idea

Use Appendix E to create a white board or PowerPoint presentation called "Christ Event Mapping." Use this for review.

6. What Christ did parallels what happens to believers. When Christ died on the cross, we died with Him. When He was buried in the grave, our old nature was buried with Him. ("Note that Paul did not write, 'we were buried *like* him,' but 'buried *with* him.'"[56]) When He was raised from the grave, we were raised to walk in new life. When He ascended into heaven, we were also seated in heavenly places with Him (Eph. 1:3; 2:6). What Christ did, He did for us. He was our substitute. In Christ, I am dead, buried, risen, and glorified. I have a whole new identity and life in Him.

7. Paul maps the Christ Event to the situation at Rome. We have already seen this in Paul's equal basis theology (Ro. 3:21-25). We may represent this in a graphical form below:

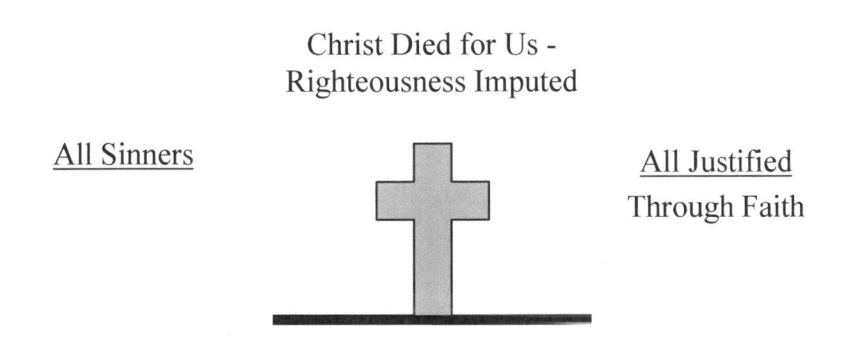

Christ Died for Us -
Righteousness Imputed

All Sinners   ✝   All Justified
Through Faith

In a very real sense, Paul's teaching on righteousness derives from Christ Event mapping. Paul takes this teaching and directly applies it to the equal basis theology, which in turn supports Paul's reconciling purpose between the two groups.

---

[56] G. Hawthorne, R. Martin, D. Reid, editors, *Dictionary of Paul and His Letters* (Downers Grove: InterVarsity Press, 1993) 62.

8. Paul continues his arguments along similar lines in Romans 8. Our whole ability to live a new life is made possible because we have died and risen in Christ: "Through Christ Jesus the law of the Spirit has set me free from the law of sin and death" (Ro. 8:2) and now "if Christ is in you, your body is dead because of sin, yet your spirit is alive because of righteousness" (Ro. 8:10). Application of the Christ Event provides all we need for this life and the next.

10

Christ Event Mapping to Our Lives

1. THE EXTENSIVE VERBAL MAP that Paul lays out in Romans 6-8 provides the spiritual milestones necessary to guide us on our daily Christian journey. Not only can we apply the Christ Event to the specific situation at Rome (showing our equal basis in Christ and the habits of the new life in the Spirit apart from law, therefore leading Jew and Gentile to accept each other), but the Christ Event provides direction for overcoming a variety of struggles.

2. Since we are united with Christ in His death, burial, and resurrection, Paul gives us clues to the process of overcoming the constant pull of sin (Ro. 7:7-8:4). He uses the language of surrender (the language of Christ's Passion): "count yourselves dead to sin;" "do not let sin reign," "do not offer the parts of your body to sin," "offer the parts of your body to him as instruments of righteousness" (Ro. 6:11-13), "offer [the parts of your body] in slavery to righteousness leading to holiness" (Ro. 6:19), and keep your "mind set on what the Spirit desires" (Ro. 8:5). The Holy Spirit brings this about in our lives, giving us the ability to "put to death the misdeeds of the body" (Ro. 8:13).

3. To take a brief, but specific example, Paul clearly maps the Christ Event to the problem of larceny in Ephesians 4:28. Here Paul admonishes the thief to stop stealing (which is the putting

to death of this sin), to work with his hands (which is the putting on of new life), and to learn to give (which seems to be the ascension aspect). It is often not sufficient to apply only the "putting off" aspect, but we must also apply the "putting on" aspects of Christ Event mapping as well. Many try to simply stop stealing, shoplifting, and so on, but if they never put on the habits of hard work and giving, then they will most likely fail.

4. Although Paul wrote more fluidly when applying the Christ Event, we could diagram each aspect as follows:

Crucified	Dead	Buried	Risen	Ascended
← Put Off →			← Put On →	
Eph. 4:28 – Stop Stealing			Work with Hands	Learn to Give

5. To apply this to another problem, we could map the solution to the lust of pornography as follows:

Crucified	Dead	Buried	Risen	Ascended
← Put Off →			← Put On →	
Stop Viewing Pornography	Stop Dwelling on the Desires	Desire Given Up	Thinking About the Opposite Sex as the Bible Directs	Praying for Those Caught in the Pornographic Industry

6. Christ's death, burial, and resurrection dealt the death blow to the control of sin in our lives. Through faith, prayer, and the working of the Holy Spirit, we can appropriate many of the benefits of the new life now. Whatever the need, Christ is the answer!

11

What about Israel?

1. PAUL CONTINUES HIS DISCOURSE with the Jewish Christians in chapters 9-11:10. Here he addresses the remaining issues and questions that the Jewish Christians would have raised against Paul's gospel. The first issue occurs in Romans 9:6, and we will put it as a question: "If being a Jew makes no difference, haven't the promises to Israel failed?" Paul answers that being an Israelite is not by natural descent, but by being selected as a child of promise.

This brings up the subsequent issue of election, and the next question, "Is God unjust?" (Ro. 9:14). Paul swiftly responds with his familiar and definitive "By no means!" followed by an explanation of God's mercy. (Behind his thinking seems to be the idea that we all deserve wrath, but it is by the mercy of God that any are saved [vs. 22].)

Whenever the issue of divine election comes up, someone always asks, "Then why does God still blame us? For who resists His will?" (Ro. 9:19). To this Paul responds that God is God. (Paul has already made the point that divine prerogative is based on foreknowledge [Ro. 8:29-30].)

There follows a litany of Old Testament Scriptures showing how God planned to include the Gentiles and left only a remnant of natural Israel to be saved. Paul concludes that the Gentiles received righteousness by faith, while in contrast, the Israelites failed to find righteousness because they pursued it by works (vs. 32). They ran hard, but stumbled over the "stumbling stone" (Ro. 9:30-33)—faith in Christ and the cross (1 Cor. 1:23).

His thoughts flow over into chapter ten, where Paul again reveals his heart's desire for the salvation of Israel (vs. 1-3).

2. Paul returns to the issue of the law in chapter 10, beginning in verse 4: "Christ is the end of the law so that there may be righteousness for everyone who believes." He explains that righteousness is by faith, not works (as though we really could bring Christ down from heaven or up from the dead, vs. 6-7). He reiterates the equal basis theology in verse 12: "For there is no difference between Jew and Gentile—the same Lord is Lord of all and richly blesses all who call on him…"

3. In chapter 10:16 through chapter 11, Paul explains that "not all the Israelites accepted the good news" and again picks up the concept that only a remnant of Israelites will be saved. He does this in answer to the next logical questions, "Did God reject his people?" (Ro. 11:1) and "Did they stumble so as to fall beyond recovery?" (Ro. 11:11). (Again his answer to each is, "By no means!")

Just as there had always been a remnant of true believers in the Old Testament, so there existed a remnant in Paul's day (Ro. 11:1-4). This remnant consisted of all the objects of God's mercy, "not only from the Jews but also from the Gentiles" (Ro. 9:24). Election to this remnant depended upon God's purpose (Ro. 9:11) and not works (Ro. 9:12, 32). Here again, Paul demonstrated his overall purpose: to establish the equal basis of Jews and Gentiles before God.

4. Paul uses the illustration of branches being broken off or grafted in to explain how Jews and Gentiles become a part of the people of God. As he does so, Paul turns his attention back to the Gentiles and warns them not to "be arrogant, but be afraid. For if God did not spare the natural branches, he will not spare you either" (vs. 20-21). They must remember that it was for their sake that the natural branches were broken off.

Israel experienced a "hardening in part until the full number of Gentiles" had come in (vs. 25).

5. The rejection of Christ by the Jews brought salvation to the Gentiles. The reception of Christ by the Gentiles would stir the Jews to receive Him. Paul's thesis that began as "first to the Jews, then to the Gentiles" had come full circle. The result is that all Israel—true Israel—Jews and Gentiles who believe in Christ—would be saved (Ro.11:26).

6. Paul summarizes his equal basis theology one last time: "For God has bound all men over to disobedience so that he may have mercy on them all" (vs. 32). He then breaks into spontaneous praise for the depths of God's riches and the mysteries of His purpose (Ro. 11:33-36). Has theology ever led you into worship?

Teaching Idea

Use Appendix F to create a white board or PowerPoint presentation called "God's Plan for the Jews." Use this for review.

12

Contemporary Relevance – Racial Reconciliation

1. WE HAVE SEEN that significant New Testament material dealt with one of the greatest challenges facing the early church: reconciliation and integration of Jewish Christians and Gentile Christians in the one body of Christ. We have also seen that Paul intended to carefully explain his gospel within the larger need for this cohesion in the community of faith at Rome. Unity of Jewish Christians and Gentile Christians was on Paul's heart (Ro. 15:6). The ground of that unity—the foundation of reconciliation—stemmed from the equal basis of all believers (Jews and Gentiles) in Christ. This means that regardless of race, all believers are placed into the body of Christ "on equal standing, with equal privileges, and of equal importance before God."[57]

The reconciliation message of Paul's epistle to the Romans has, therefore, much to offer us today. If we are equally lost and equally indebted to Christ for salvation, do we have any basis for being judgmental of each other, let alone of another race? Is there any room for boasting? For Paul, the answer would be an unequivocal "No!" If we are the one body of Christ and dependent on the gifts of one another, how can we maintain

---

[57] Larry Mercer, *A Biblical and Cultural Study of the Problem of Racism*, **Bibliotheca Sacra**, vol. 153, no. 609, Jan. 1996, 90.

racial boundaries any longer? Is not our identity in Christ far more important than ethnicity and passing culture?

2. The epistle of Paul to the Romans does not tolerate the idea of "separate but equal." Segregation was fuel for the Judaizer's match. As Francis Watson has pointed out, the "purpose of welcoming or receiving one another is common worship"[58] (Ro. 14:1; 15:6-12). Learning to worship together is a key to unity. We must learn to worship together and celebrate the rich diversity of music and liturgy of every culture. To make this possible, we must tear down any attitude or practice that maintains a barrier between the races.

Worship styles such as rocking and swaying to black gospel music or shouting an "Amen" in dialogue with the preacher are culturally disputable matters and not to be judged. Too often we preach culture as doctrine from our pulpits, thus polarizing the churches along racial lines. It is possible to worship in a different manner without compromising one's beliefs. Christianity is not bound by specific forms of cultural expression.

3. But can we do more than acknowledge our unity? Should we not look for opportunities to unite racial factions as Paul did with the offering from the Gentiles for the Jews? Paul accepted personal responsibility to build a bridge between the two races—a responsibility from which he refused to be deterred and that would eventually cost him his life. Should we be any less intentional? Churches that break down comfort barriers by hosting unity services among diverse churches display this kind of intentionality.

If God is impartial, should we be any less equitable in rendering opportunities to minorities? Should not the "strong" (privileged) take the initiative and deny themselves? Is it not up to them to limit their liberty? F. F. Bruce commented: "No Christian was more thoroughly emancipated than Paul, but

---

[58] Francis Watson, *The Two Roman Congregations*, in *The Romans Debate*, 206.

none was readier to limit his own liberty in the interests of his fellow Christians."[59] There can no longer be reluctance on the part of one group to share ecclesiastical authority with another group.

Has not racial separation between churches hindered the spread of the gospel message today just as it could have in Paul's time? Does not racial prejudice in the Church make it difficult for some to be saved?

4. In a day when Sunday morning still remains the most segregated hour of the week, we should turn to the racial reconciliation message of Paul's epistle to the Romans for principles to guide us. Our nation still gropes for solutions to racial problems stemming from the blight of slavery and the maltreatment of Native Americans and other minorities. I believe there are both practical and theological solutions to the problem of racism to be found in Paul's epistle—surely ample guidance to bring reconciliation to the Church in the United States.

For all the systematic theology that Romans has provided the Church, why has not the reconciliation message also reached the trenches? The United States has experienced rapid multi-cultural change, but much segregation and prejudice still exists. The racial reconciliation message of Paul's epistle to the Romans is urgently needed today.

Teaching Idea

Do a class exercise. Write a three-page "autobiography" as a fictional member of a Roman congregation that includes your reaction (positively or negatively) to Paul's letter.

---

[59] Bruce, *The Romans Debate*, 186.

Paul's Character

13

Paul's Character

1. WE HAVE SEEN how Paul's epistle to the Romans gives us a view into the situation at Rome—the division and prejudice—and how Paul sought to bring the Jewish and Gentile Christians together. We have noted Paul's deep understanding of theology that under girded his practical solutions throughout the epistle. We have also seen his apostolic goals to evangelize Spain. Beyond this background situation, purpose, and theological content, however, the epistle gives us an unmatched glimpse into the character of this man.

2. Unlike his other epistles, Paul sent this one to a congregation he had never visited. Consequently, we see Paul at his diplomatic best, drawing the two factions together with a careful balance of correction, appeal, and discussion. For example, Paul maintained a love and genuine concern for his Jewish race (Ro. 3:9, 19; 9:3; 10:1), while unhesitatingly reprimanding their hypocrisy and pride (Ro. 2:17-24; 3:27-30).

3. Paul was not ashamed to speak the truth—whether theological truth or truth necessary for correction (Ro. 2:1-6). He lit the match of truth to the spiritual dead wood in the hearts of many. Yet he remained vulnerable and understood his own frailties (Ro. 7:14). In Romans 7:7-25, his words reflect a personal encounter with the struggles of temptation and sin. Throughout the epistle one senses a man devoted to the efficacy of what he wrote.

4. What he wrote revealed a deep commitment to Christ and gratitude for His redeeming work (Ro. 5:1-11). What he wrote reveals the culmination of years of labor to establish the fledgling churches. It also shows the refined debate with the Judaizers or synagogue Jews. In addition, he wrote keenly aware of the far-reaching affects of the Christ event and their application to the needs at hand. He was articulate and intelligent, showing an amazing grasp of the Old Testament Scriptures and a clear understanding of the freedom of new life in Christ.

5. F. F. Bruce called Paul, "the apostle of the heart set free" (2 Cor. 3:17) and we should not overlook this dimension of Paul's character in Romans (cf. Ro. 8:2). Paul identified with the strong of conscience, who no longer felt personally constrained by religious scruples. Christ changed Paul from the meticulous Jew who strove with zeal to keep every single law into the liberated teacher who could pronounce that Christ was the "end of the law" (Ro. 10:4). In this radical declaration we see clearly the heart of an emancipated Jew! Nevertheless, the ever-pragmatic Paul restrained his liberties for the sake of the gospel (cf. Ro. 14:14, 20) and out of respect for the weaker consciences of other believers.

6. What do we make of this man called Paul? We could say without reservation that he lived for the Kingdom of God. Indeed, one could say he felt wholly obligated and burdened with the need to preach the gospel (Ro. 1:14; 8:12). He was once the worst of sinners who became the best of apostles. Though he would eventually arrive at Rome in chains, his epistle will endure to set the captives free!

Teaching Idea

As a final class exercise, work together to write a diatribe drama between the Christian Jews and Gentiles with Paul as the mediator between them. Use the questions and answers in Paul's epistle and try to reproduce the conversation and attitude of each faction. (For example, students one year wrote a skit called "Espresso Romano" that used Paul's diatribe in a modern café setting.)

Appendix A: Overview

This appendix contains the Class Handout and Presentation Steps for presenting an overview of the chapters in Romans.

Appendix A

Presentation Steps

Slide 1

> # Overview of Paul's Epistle to the Romans
>
> Chapter Breakout

Slide 2

> # Overview of Romans
>
> Chapter Breakout
>
> | Ro. 1: 1-17 | | Ro. 15: 14-33 | |
> |---|---|---|---|
>
> - In these verses Paul addresses his epistle to the Romans and frames his epistle with explanations for writing it.

Slide 3

Overview of Romans

Chapter Breakout

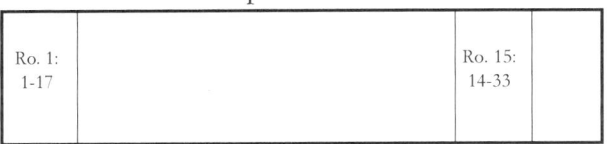

Ro. 1: 1-17		Ro. 15: 14-33	

- These verses also express Paul's desire to see them and to have them pray for him. Further, they contain Paul's thesis for the letter (Ro. 1:14-17).

Slide 4

Overview of Romans

Chapter Breakout

Ro. 1: 1-17		Ro. 15: 14-33	Ro. 16

- Chapter 16 contains Paul's personal greetings to the Jewish Christian and Gentile Christian groups at Rome. We can identify at least five separate home groups divided between Jews and Gentiles.

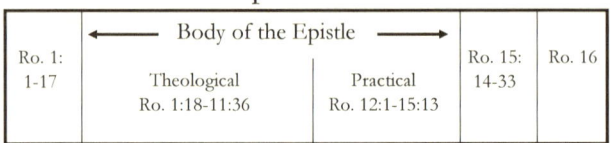

Appendix A

Slide 5

Overview of Romans

Chapter Breakout

Ro. 1: 1-17	← Body of the Epistle →		Ro. 15: 14-33	Ro. 16
	Theological Ro. 1:18-11:36	Practical Ro. 12:1-15:13		

- The body of the epistle contains two lengthy discussions, one largely theological (Ro. 1:8-11:36), and the other largely practical (Ro. 12:1-15:13).

Slide 6

Overview of Romans

Chapter Breakout

Ro. 1: 1-17	← Body of the Epistle →		Ro. 15: 14-33	Ro. 16
	Theological Ro. 1:18-11:36	Practical Ro. 12:1-15:13		

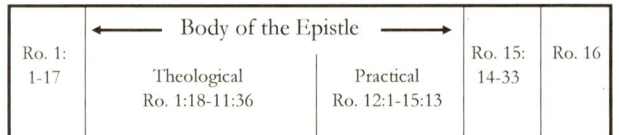

- Both the theological and practical content address the immediate situation at Rome by applying Paul's gospel to reconcile the Jew and Gentile Christians.

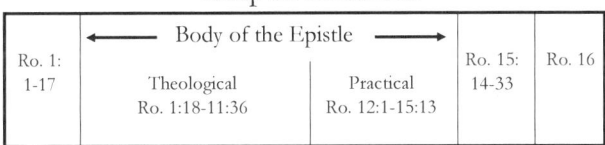

Romans and Reconciliation

Slide 7

Overview of Romans

Chapter Breakout

Ro. 1: 1-17	← Body of the Epistle →		Ro. 15: 14-33	Ro. 16
	Theological Ro. 1:18-11:36	Practical Ro. 12:1-15:13		

- For instance, the theological section ends with the climactic summary of equality: "For God has bound all men over to disobedience so that he may have mercy on them all" (Ro. 11:32).

Slide 8

Overview of Romans

Chapter Breakout

Ro. 1: 1-17	← Body of the Epistle →		Ro. 15: 14-33	Ro. 16
	Theological Ro. 1:18-11:36	Practical Ro. 12:1-15:13		

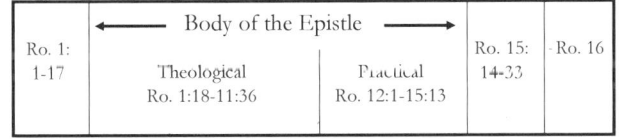

- The practical section contains a series of admonitions seeking to draw the two groups together in love and worship.

Appendix A

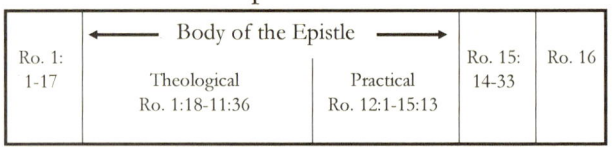

Slide 9

Overview of Romans

Chapter Breakout

Ro. 1: 1-17	← Body of the Epistle →		Ro. 15: 14-33	Ro. 16
	Theological Ro. 1:18-11:36	Practical Ro. 12:1-15:13		

- Romans was designed to head off the Judaizers and prepare the Romans to help him for future missions into Spain.

Slide 10

Overview of Romans

Chapter Breakout

Ro. 1: 1-17	← Body of the Epistle →		Ro. 15: 14-33	Ro. 16
	Theological Ro. 1:18-11:36	Practical Ro. 12:1-15:13		

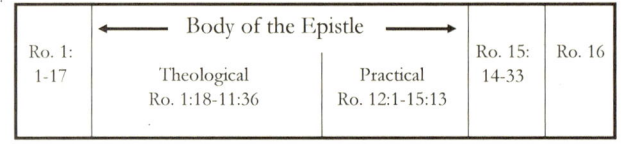

- Romans is the culmination of Paul's theology and a masterpiece of Spirit-inspired literature.

Overview of Romans

Chapter Breakout

Appendix A

Appendix B: Background

The following are suggested presentation points for creating a "Background Situation of Romans" PowerPoint presentation.

Presentation Steps

Slide 1

Background Situation

- Paul desired to visit Rome for some time (Ro. 1:10-13; 15:23; Acts 19:21).
- Paul planned to open missions into Spain and have the Roman Christians assist him (Ro. 15:23-24; cf. 2 Cor. 10:16).
- However, Paul must first deliver the offering from the Gentile Christians to the Jews at Jerusalem (Ro. 15:25-28).

Slide 2

Background Situation

- Paul knew that this delay could mean that the legalistic views of the Judaizers might arrive in Rome ahead of Paul (Ro. 16:17).
- He also knew that the Church in Rome was largely divided among Jewish and Gentile Christian groups (Ro. 16).
- This division was partly the result of the expulsion of the Jewish community under Emperor Claudius in A.D. 49.

Slide 3

Background Situation

- Since Paul could not travel to Rome immediately, he did the next best thing—he sent them a lengthy epistle.
- This epistle needed to contain a comprehensive explanation of Paul's gospel—contra the Judaizers, and a clear explanation of the gospel's effects on the relationship between Jews and Gentiles.

Slide 4

Background Situation

- Paul's epistle to the Romans is therefore preemptive and reconciling in its overall purpose.
- Paul used practical and theological countermeasures to reconcile the two groups.
- Paul addressed each group in turn, leveling the ground by the gospel, and encouraging them to worship together.

Slide 5

Background Situation

- Thus, Paul faced one of the most difficult challenges ever to face the Church: reconciliation and integration of Jewish and Gentile Christians in the one body of Christ. His answer was the masterpiece we call Romans.

Appendix C: The Law

The following are suggested presentation points for creating a "Romans and the Law" PowerPoint presentation.

Presentation Steps

Slide 1

Romans and the Law

- Paul clearly states that all are sinners with or without the Law (Ro. 2:12) and that righteousness is by faith apart from the Law (Ro. 3:21, 28). He thus levels the ground between Jewish and Gentile Christians.

Slide 2

Romans and the Law

- In leveling the ground between these groups at Rome, Paul must answer the questions that would have been foremost on the minds of the Jewish Christians: "If we do come to Christ the same as Gentiles, then why did God give us the Law? What is its purpose, if it doesn't provide righteousness?"

Slide 3

Romans and the Law

- Over the course of Romans, Paul spells out the purpose and function of the Law:
  - It defines sin and awakens the conscience to sin (Ro. 3:20). Paul put it this way: "where there is no law there is no transgression" (Ro. 4:15; 5:13b).
  - It declares everyone a sinner. "The law was added so that the trespass might increase" (Ro. 5:20).

Slide 4

Romans and the Law

- The law declares the penalty for each kind of sin. Paul said that it condemns those who disobey it (Ro. 5:18) and that it "brings wrath" (Ro. 4:15).

- In some ways the law is designed to prevent sin, but because of the sin nature, the law actually multiplies it. It intensifies the desire for sin because it stirs up the sense of sin (Ro. 3:19-20; 7:7-25).

Slide 5

Romans and the Law

- The Law is "holy, righteous, and good" (Ro. 7:12). The problem lies with us.
- The only way to overcome sin is to die to it (in Christ) and receive the life of the Spirit. The only way to fulfill the law is to die to it thereby coming out from under its condemnation, sin force, and yoke of works/righteousness.
- Our relationship to the Law has now changed. We have been set free to obey the righteous requirements of the law through the enablement of the Spirit, not through works of the flesh (Ro. 7:6).

Slide 6

Romans and the Law

- In no uncertain terms, Paul declares that our relationship to the Law is now radically changed:
  - We are dead to the Law (Ro. 7:4).
  - We are released from the Law (Ro. 7:6).
  - We are set free from the Law (Ro. 8:2).
  - Christ is the end of the Law (Ro. 10:4).
- We now have the power of the Spirit to overcome the power of the flesh, something the Law could not do.

Appendix D: Principles

The following are suggested presentation points for creating a "Moral Absolutes and Principles" PowerPoint presentation.

Appendix D

Presentation Steps

Slide 1

> # Moral Absolutes and Principles
>
> Romans 14:13-15:1

Slide 2

> # Moral Absolutes and Principles
>
> - Every Biblical principle has as its basis the *two moral absolutes:*
>   - Moral Absolute #1 - <u>Love God</u>.
>   - Moral Absolute #2 - <u>Love One Another</u>.
>
>   (Deut. 6:4-5; Lev. 19:18; Mt. 22:36-40; Jn. 13:34-35; Gal. 5:13-14)

Slide 3

Moral Absolutes and Principles

- The two absolutes are interrelated. You cannot say you love God and hate your brother (1 Jn. 4:19-21). You cannot say you love God and walk in sin.
- Further, Christ defined both kinds of love in His Person and actions: "Love one another *as I have loved you*" (Jn. 13:34).

Slide 4

Moral Absolutes and Principles

- Laws and commands in Scripture are nothing more than restatements of the two moral absolutes to a specific situation.
- Paul states this in Ro 13:8-10: "Let no debt remain outstanding, except the continuing debt to love one another, for he who loves his fellowman has fulfilled the law. The commandments, 'Do not commit adultery,' 'Do not murder,' 'Do not steal,' 'Do not covet,' and whatever other commandment there may be, are summed up in this one rule: 'Love your neighbor as yourself.' Love does no harm to its neighbor. Therefore love is the fulfillment of the law." (See Ex. 20:13-15,17; Deut. 5:17-19, 21; Lev. 19:18.)

Appendix D

Slide 5

Moral Absolutes and Principles

- Principles are universal truths succinctly stated. Principles are timeless. They make sense in any culture at any time.
- Principles bridge the gap between the "then and now." They make the truths of the Bible relevant in our present culture.

Slide 6

Moral Absolutes and Principles

- Sometimes the Bible states the principle for us. Sometimes we must read a story, parable, or prophecy and find the principle in the text.
- Such is the case with the principle "you reap what you sow," which is one of the oldest known principles (see Job 4:8). (See also Job 4:8; Ps. 126:5; Prov. 22:8; Eccl. 11:4; Hos. 8:7,10:12; 1 Cor. 9:11; 2 Cor. 9:6; and Gal. 6:7-9.)

Slide 7

Moral Absolutes and Principles

- Often the laws and commands of Scripture have cultural particulars. Even the Ten Commandments have some cultural particulars in them (Deut. 5:7-21).
- Finding the principles for today may require separating the cultural particulars and observing the principles closer to the two moral absolutes.

Slide 8

Moral Absolutes and Principles

- Let's look at the two absolutes and several principles that Paul uses in Romans 14:13- 15:1 and how he applies them to the situation at Rome.

Appendix D

Slide 9

Romans 14:13-15:1

Love God   Love One Another

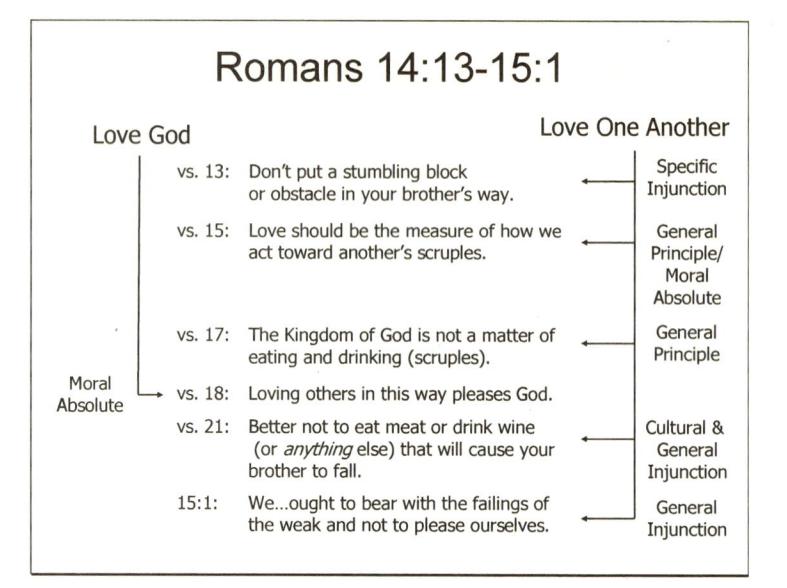

vs. 13:	Don't put a stumbling block or obstacle in your brother's way.	Specific Injunction
vs. 15:	Love should be the measure of how we act toward another's scruples.	General Principle/ Moral Absolute
vs. 17:	The Kingdom of God is not a matter of eating and drinking (scruples).	General Principle
vs. 18:	Loving others in this way pleases God.	*(Moral Absolute)*
vs. 21:	Better not to eat meat or drink wine (or *anything* else) that will cause your brother to fall.	Cultural & General Injunction
15:1:	We...ought to bear with the failings of the weak and not to please ourselves.	General Injunction

Slide 10

Moral Absolutes and Principles

- Paul applies the two moral absolutes to the specific needs of the Roman Christians.
- He shows us principles for living even though we may not have the specific problem of eating meat or drinking wine in a manner that would offend the scruples of the Jewish Christians. (Probably food and drink offered to idols. See 1 Cor. 8.)

Appendix E: Christ Event

The following are suggested presentation points for creating a "Christ Event Mapping" PowerPoint presentation.

Appendix E

Presentation Steps

Slide 1

Christ Event Mapping

Applying the Drama of the Gospel

Slide 2

Christ Event Mapping

- The gospel is the whole drama of the Christ Event from crucifixion to ascension—from the cross to the throne. Whether dealing with doctrine or practical application, Paul returned to the Christ Event for the answer.
- In the same way, it is imperative that we understand each step of the Christ Event *and its significance* so that we can adjust our thinking and apply the truth of the gospel to our lives.

Slide 3

Christ Event Mapping

CHRIST

Death → Burial → Resurrection → Ascension

BELIEVER

Dead in Christ
Ro. 6:5-8, 11

Buried with Christ
Ro. 6:3-4

Raised with Christ
Ro. 6:4-5, 13
Ro. 7:4-6

Glorified
Ro. 8:30

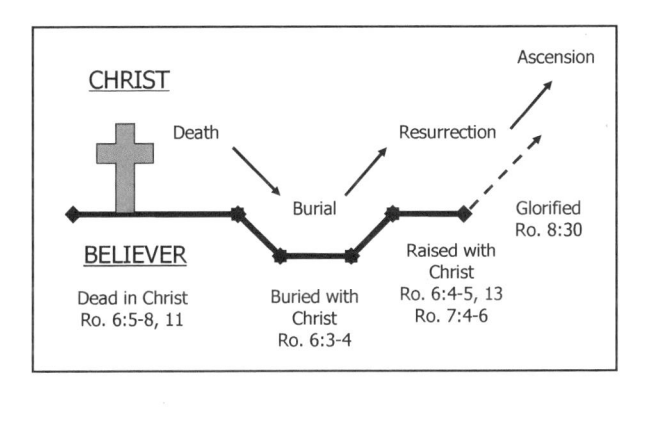

Slide 4

Christ Event Mapping

- This simple map shows a parallel track for what Christ did and what has happened to a believer.
- When Christ died on the cross, we died with Him.
- When He was buried in the grave, our old nature was buried with Him.
- When He was raised from the grave, we were raised to walk in newness of life.
- When He ascended into heaven, we were also seated in heavenly places with Him (Eph. 1:3; 2:6).

Appendix E

Slide 5

Christ Event Mapping

- What Christ did, He did for us. He was our substitute. In Christ, I am dead, buried, risen, and glorified. I have a whole new identity and life in Him.
- Because of the significance of our identity in Christ, Paul consistently returned to the Christ Event to offer solutions to the needs existing in each of the fledgling churches.

Slide 6

Christ Event Mapping

- For instance, to the Galatians (Gal. 2:11-21; 3:13, 26-29; 6:15-16), Ephesians (Eph. 2:13-16), and Romans (Ro. 3) Paul refers to the affects of the Christ Event at reconciling Jews and Gentiles, a persistent problem in first century Christianity.

Slide 7

Christ Event Mapping

- To the Ephesians Paul spells out the necessity of putting off the old nature and putting on the new (Christ Event mapping) in the context of overcoming an assortment of sins including deceitful desires, falsehood, and anger (Eph. 2:20-23).

Slide 8

Christ Event Mapping

- When Paul wrote of living by the Spirit in Galatians and Romans, he grounded the new life in the Christ Event:
  - Those who belong to Christ Jesus have crucified the sinful nature with its passions and desires. —Gal. 5:24
  - We were therefore buried with him through baptism into death in order that, just as Christ was raised from the dead through the glory of the Father, we too may live a new life.—Ro. 6:4

Appendix E

Slide 9

Christ Event Mapping

- To the Colossians Paul again maps the Christ Event to dispel the condemnation of those who tried to place them under the Law (Col. 2:2-23):
    - In him you were also circumcised, in the putting off of the sinful nature, not with a circumcision done by the hands of men but with the circumcision done by Christ, having been buried with him in baptism and raised with him through your faith in the power of God, who raised him from the dead.—Col. 2:11-12

Slide 10

Christ Event Mapping

- When Paul comforted the Thessalonians with the promise of Christ's return (1 Thess. 4:13ff), he grounded it in the death and life of Christ (1 Thess. 5:10).
- To Timothy Paul recited an early formula of the gospel: "If we died with him, we will also live with him; If we endure, we will also reign with him" (2 Tim. 2:11-12). He then applies it in a practical way (2 Ti. 2:14).

Slide 11

Christ Event Mapping

- When Paul talks about putting the earthly nature to death (Ro. 6:11; 8:13; Col. 3:5), he is referring to mapping the Christ Event to our lives.
- To the Philippians (Phil. 3:19-20) and the Colossians (Col. 3:1-3) Paul maps the ascension aspect of the Christ Event to our ability to set our minds on things above.

Slide 12

Christ Event Mapping

- The Corinthians probably took the ascension aspects of the Christ Event to an extreme, believing that they were already resurrected (and consequently that there was no resurrection to come; 1 Cor. 15:12). To this Paul carefully explains the future resurrection and the balance between the natural and spiritual bodies (1 Cor. 15:35ff; cf. 2 Cor. 5:1-10).

Slide 13

Christ Event Mapping

- Paul has Christ Event mapping in mind when he declares to the Corinthians that "if anyone is in Christ, he is a new creation" (2 Cor. 5:17) and that "God made him to be sin for us" (2 Cor. 5:21). As such "we regard no one from a worldly point of view" (2 Cor. 5:16).

Slide 14

Christ Event Mapping

- In fact, one of Paul's favorite phrases succinctly expresses Christ Event mapping: that we are "in Christ." (See Ro. 6:11; 8:1; 1 Cor. 1:30; 15:22; Phil 3:14; Col. 2:9-10 and so on; or "through" Christ Jesus, Ro. 7:25).
- In addition, Paul connects other terms to Christ Event mapping. For example, we are "co-heirs" *with* Christ (Ro. 8:17) if we *share* in his sufferings (Ro. 8:12-17).

Slide 15

Christ Event Mapping

- In short, all our relationships are now affected by our identity in Christ (Gal. 3:28).
- It would not be an understatement to say that the gospel is the core of Paul's theology, but that core is not just "good news," it is the application of the entire Christ Event to our lives.

Appendix E

Appendix F: God's Plan

The following are suggested presentation points for creating a "God's Plan for the Jews" PowerPoint presentation.

Appendix F

Presentation Steps

Slide 1

God's Plan for the Jews

Romans 9-11

Slide 2

God's Plan for the Jews

- In Romans 9-11 Paul returns to a question he first raised in chapter three: since we all come to Christ the same way, "What advantage, then, is there in being a Jew?"
- To this question Paul adds two more, "Did Israel not understand?" (Ro. 10:18-19) and "Did God reject his people?" (Ro. 11:1).
- As a Jew, Paul has certainly pondered these tough questions many times. In these three chapters he offers us profound insights into God's plan.

Slide 3

God's Plan for the Jews

- Paul begins by listing the eightfold advantage of the nation of Israel (Ro. 9:4-5). Theirs is the:
  - Adoption as Sons
  - Divine Glory
  - Covenants
  - Receiving of the Law
  - Temple Worship
  - Promises
  - Patriarchs
  - Human Ancestry of Christ

Slide 4

God's Plan for the Jews

- Despite this advantage, the Jews failed to obtain righteousness because they sought it not by faith. They pursued the right thing the wrong way.
- Does this mean that God is finished with the nation of Israel? Paul's answer is to point to himself. He is part of a remnant "chosen by grace."

Slide 5

God's Plan for the Jews

- Here we begin to glimpse God's plan. God reserves a remnant of the Jews at this time and in His own time He will return to the nation as a whole.
- The failure of the Jews has brought "riches for the Gentiles" (Ro. 11:12). In other words, because the Jews in large part rejected Christ, the gospel message was delivered to the Gentiles.

Slide 6

God's Plan for the Jews

- "Israel has experienced a hardening in part until the full number of Gentiles has come in" (Ro. 11:25).
- In turn, because the Gentiles received mercy, the Jews will be provoked to envy and salvation (Ro. 11:11, 14).
- Upon concluding his thoughts about God's plan, Paul breaks out in worship: His paths are beyond searching out (Ro. 11:33-36)!

Slide 7

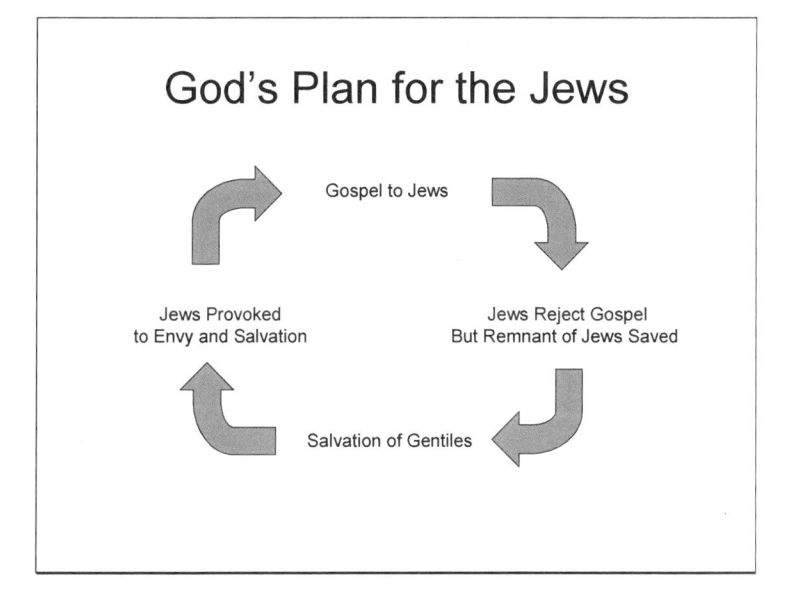

God's Plan for the Jews

Gospel to Jews

Jews Reject Gospel
But Remnant of Jews Saved

Salvation of Gentiles

Jews Provoked
to Envy and Salvation

Appendix F

Appendix G: The Jew/Gentile Racial Setting of the New Testament

Introduction

To the Jews, God divided the world between themselves—His chosen people—and everyone else. The Jews believed their staunch separation as a unique people to be part and parcel to remaining holy before God. (In this regard, race and religion are inextricably intertwined.) This separation was marked by circumcision, which identified them as part of the Abrahamic covenant and recipients of God's Law and Promised Land.

To the Gentiles (Greeks or Hellenists), one either embraced Hellenism (Greek language, religion, culture, and philosophy) or else one was ostracized as a barbarian.[60] In large part, the Greek and Roman Gentiles believed it their duty to force Hellenism on conquered peoples.

These diametrically opposing viewpoints resulted in a "dividing wall of hostility" (Eph. 2:14) that was exacerbated by the rule of first Greeks, then (Hellenistic) Romans in Palestine. Consequently, Jews and Gentiles mingled and clashed in significant ways in the First Century Mediterranean world.[61]

Into this volatile mix came a man from Galilee—a remote part of the Greco-Roman world—with a message that included racial

---

[60] Although numerous other cultures vied for dominance in the First Century Mediterranean world, Hellenism was by far the greatest and, therefore, the focus of this paper. "Gentiles" refers loosely to "Hellenists" in this paper. "Barbarian" (Acts 28:2) is an onomatopoeic word given by the Greeks for other "uncivilized" languages that sound so much like "bar-bar-bar." See Robert Picirilli, *Paul the Apostle* (Chicago: Moody Press, 1986), 14. Interestingly, both Jews and Greeks called each other atheists.

[61] That this distinction between Jews and Gentiles was based not only on social and religious differences, but also on differences of race, can be clearly demonstrated in the writings of Paul (e.g. Ro. 9:3-8; 11:1; Col. 3:11).

Appendix G

reconciliation. From the start, Jesus broke down the barriers between Jews and Gentiles (Mk. 7:14-15, 19).[62] And although He ministered first to Jews (Mt. 10:5-6; 15:21-28), He later commissioned His followers to "make disciples of all nations" (πάντα τὰ ἔθνη, Mt. 28:19) and to be witnesses in "Samaria, and to the ends of the earth" (Acts 1:8; cf. Mt. 21:13; Jn. 10:16).[63] To fulfill His "Great Commission" meant that racial issues had to be met head on.

How could these races be reconciled? How did the Jew/Gentile relationship affect Christians? Would Gentile Christians have to first become Jews? The purpose of this appendix is to answer these questions by giving an overview of the Jew/Gentile racial setting of the First Century Mediterranean world and by giving an overview of the related Jew/Gentile racial issues addressed in the New Testament. The first part defines Judaism and Hellenism, gives an overview of various Jewish groups and how they interacted, and examines evidence of racial segregation, prejudice, and strife. The second part looks briefly at the Jew/Gentile relationship in the books of Acts, Romans, Galatians, and Ephesians, giving special emphasis to the impact of the Judaizers on this relationship.

An Overview of the Jew/Gentile Racial Setting in the First Century

This section broadly defines Judaism and Hellenism, examines the history of strife between their adherents, and examines the racial segregation and prejudice that underpins much of that relationship.

---

[62] See J. Andrew Kirk, "Race, Class, Caste and the Bible," *Themelios* 10, (Jan. 1985): 12.

[63] On the ethnic significance of Acts 1:8, see "'To the End of the Earth': The Geographical and Ethnic Universalism of Acts 1:8 in Light of Isaianic Influence on Luke," *Journal of the Evangelical Theological Society* 40 (September 1997): 389-399. The commission to include the Gentiles can also be seen in Christ's prediction of Matthew 10:18 and 24:9 (cf. Mt. 22:8-10; 21:40-46). The Gospel of Matthew, though written primarily to Jews, also included many positive accounts toward Gentiles (Matt. 2:1–12; 8:5–13; 12:14–21; 15:21–28).

Jews/Judaism

Although one must not characterize Judaism as monolithic,[64] three things in common constitute Judaism: social laws, religious beliefs (including circumcision, the Sabbath, the festivals and dietary laws), and ancestry/race. These three aspects of Judaism largely determined the boundaries that separated Jews from Gentiles. The term "Jew," then, ostensibly distinguished this race from all other ethnic and religious groups.

Living in the Holy Land and governing the nation was also integral to Jewish identity. Nevertheless, after the Diaspora the Jews derived their identity largely from synagogue life, which centered on the study of the Law (Acts 15:21). This remained important even during the restoration of the Temple in Jerusalem, and in fact, allowed Judaism to continue after its destruction in A.D. 70. This corporate "nomistic" identity preserved and fostered a sense of separateness from Gentiles[65] and was promoted by the scribes and rabbis who became the custodians of the Law.

Despite this common identity, however, a general difference existed between Diaspora Jews, who were scattered throughout the Roman Empire, and Palestinian Jews. The Diaspora Jews, though living largely in separate communities from Gentiles, would have been far more influenced by Hellenism than Palestinian Jews. And in terms of comparative growth, they outnumbered the Palestinian Jews by two to one.

---

[64] Despite how Paul characterized the relationship between Jews and Gentiles *in general* as hostile (τὴν ἐχθραν; Ephesians 2:11-22), the relationships between Jews and Gentiles in the Roman world were complex. See Bruce W. Fong, "Addressing the Issue of Racial Reconciliation According to the Principles of Ephesians 2:11-22," *Journal of the Evangelical Theological Society* 38 (December 1995): 565-580. Fong cites W. Rader, *The Church and Racial Hostility: A History of Interpretation of Ephesians 2:11-22* (Tubingen: J.C. B. Mohr). See also the discussion in G. Hawthorne, R. Martin, D. Reid, eds., *Dictionary of Paul and His Letters*, (Downers Grove: IVP, 1993), 335f and John G. Gager, "Judaism as Seen by Outsiders," Robert A. Kraft and George W. E. Nickelsburg, editors, *Early Judaism and Its Modern Interpreters*, (Atlanta: Scholars Press, 1986), 99-116. Also see James Dunn, *New Perspectives on Paul and the Law* (Grand Rapids: Eerdmans, 2007), 302-306.

[65] Longenecker, 31.

In contrast, most Palestinian Jews[66] "tended to be more provincial than those reared in the Dispersion, and were less likely to speak Greek."[67] Among the stricter sects of the Jews (e.g., Zealots, Pharisees, and Essenes) there was "considerable resistance to Hellenization."[68] Philo, who was deeply influenced by Greek philosophies, is often cited as an example of a Hellenistic Jew of the Diaspora. In contrast, the Apostle Peter was reared in Palestine and had less contact with Greek culture, language, and philosophy. Even after his conversion he found it difficult at times to socialize with Gentiles (cf. Acts 10; Gal. 2:11-14). Nevertheless, it remained possible for a Diaspora Jew to be thoroughly Hebraic, and a Palestinian Jew to be greatly influenced by Hellenism, though both would be the general exception.[69]

Other Jewish groups influencing the Jew/Gentile relationships included the Sadducees, a class consisting of the rich aristocracy, and whose power derived from the temple cult and political maneuverings.[70] It is not surprising, then, that after the destruction of the temple in A.D. 70, the Sadducees largely disappeared from the scene.

---

[66] Palestine of the Jews consisted of Galilee and Judea proper, but did not include Galilee of the Gentiles (Mt. 4:15). Bethsaida and Caesarea Philippi were largely Gentile cities.

[67] Picirilli, 13.

[68] Ibid.

[69] At times certain mistrust appeared between the Diaspora Jews and the Palestinian Jews. This is illustrated in the flare-up over the support of widows in Acts 6.

As a Diaspora Jew and Roman citizen (Acts 22:25-29), Paul was thoroughly acquainted with the prevailing customs of the Greco-Roman world. (See Marvin Wilson, *Our Father Abraham: Jewish Roots of the Christian Faith*, (Grand Rapids: Eerdmans, 1989), 46.) Evidently he studied the Greek philosophers since the NT records that he quoted Gentile sayings four times (Acts 17:28 (twice); 1 Cor. 15:33; and Titus 1:12). This may also illustrate a general acceptance on the part of the Diaspora Jews regarding what may be aligned with Hebrew ethics or thought. "The Hebraic opposition to enforced Hellenization does not mean an absolute antagonism to every Greek term, idea, or form of expression" (Longenecker, 57). On the other hand, Paul could claim to be a "Hebrew of Hebrews" (Phil. 3:5; cf. Acts 23:6). He was knowledgeable in the rich legacy of his people through his Pharisaic training under the famous Jewish rabban Gamaliel.

[70] See Mt. 3:7; 16:1-12; 22:23, Acts 5:17; 23:6 and Josephus, *Antiquities of the Jews*, 13.171–173, 293–298; 18.11, 16–17; 20.199.

Another group consisted of the Pharisees, whom Paul called "the strictest sect" of Judaism (Acts 26:5; the name means "separated ones").[71] "They deplored the inroads of Hellenistic ways into Jewish life under the Ptolomies and Seleucids."[72] During the persecutions under Antiochus IV (175-164 B.C.), their zeal to keep their Hebrew way of life led to a revolt that eventually won temporary independence.[73] In general, this group emphasized the letter of the Law and created many rabbinic rules that defined how one was to keep it. These rules were rejected by the Sadducees, who were also often at odds with them politically. According to Josephus, the Pharisees numbered about 6,000 during the time of Christ and were very influential.

The Pharisees and Sadducees were also involved with the early persecution of Christians (Acts 8:1-3; 9:1-2; cf. 12:1-19) as they formed the majority of members in the ruling Jewish court (or Sanhedrin) that was the instrumental institution in affecting it. Though often at odds themselves, the Pharisees and Sadducees were united in their hatred of Christians and foreigners.[74]

The Essenes were another Jewish religious group that emphasized a celibate and communal way of life. They strictly observed the Law, the Sabbath, and purification rites, and required a three-year initiation period before allowing a Jew to join the community. Josephus mentions about 4,000 men who lived this way around the time of Christ.[75]

When Christianity began to spread throughout the Mediterranean world, another significant group, known as the Judaizers, played a negative role in the relationships between Jewish and Gentile Christians. This appendix takes up the problem of the Judaizers shortly.

---

[71] Picirilli, 22.

[72] F. F. Bruce, *Paul, Apostle of the Heart Set Free* (Grand Rapids: Eerdmans, 1995), 45. The pious Pharisees were known earlier as the Hasidim, those who keep the covenant love or *hesed*. See F. F. Bruce, *New Testament History* (New York: Doubleday, 1971), 69-70.

[73] Antiochus gained their animosity by setting up Zeus worship in the temple and by forbidding Jews from practicing their religion. The liberating of the temple is commemorated in the Festival of Dedication (Hanukkah, or Feast of Lights).

[74] Edersheim, 30.

[75] Josephus, *Antiquities of the Jews*, 18.1.2.

Appendix G

Hellenists and Hellenization

Hellenization refers to the active spread of Greek language and culture, which began under Alexander the Great (circa 320 B.C.), but continued long after his death, especially among the nations controlled by the Romans. The Romans (and others) were therefore called "Hellenists," who were "people of non-Greek origin who adopt and promote Greek customs."[76]

The Hellenic way of life included Greek art, architectural designs, and buildings such as the agora, theaters, baths, gymnasiums, and temples. The latter three were probably an affront to Hebrew practice, especially the temples, and were certainly avoided by pious Jews. Hellenism also included schools of philosophy and the learning and promotion of (koine) Greek, which became the language of commerce.

Strife and Persecution

Josephus notes that the Jews had a great deal of autonomy under Roman rule[77] as long as they cooperated—and many did. However, a large, vocal group of pious Jews and Zealots resisted any compromise with rule by Rome or its Hellenization. In fact, Josephus mentions the hatred between the Jews and the Romans numerous times in *The Wars of the Jews*,[78] especially during the violent and bloody conquest of the Jews in Palestine by the Roman generals Vespasian and Titus (A.D. 67-71). Philo, a Hellenistic Jew, likewise mentioned the animosity.[79] Open conflict lasted between A.D. 66 and 73, with the final battle occurring at Masada.[80]

---

[76]Stanley E. Porter and Craig A. Evans, *Dictionary of New Testament Background : A Compendium of Contemporary Biblical Scholarship* (Downers Grove, IL: InterVarsity Press, 2000) Libronix e-book. The term "Hellenism" occurs in 2 Macc. 4:10, 13; 6:9; 11:24.

[77] Josephus, *Jewish Wars*, 6.4.2.

[78] Josephus, *Jewish Wars*, (1.1, 2.3; 2.18.8, 9; 3.7.1; 4.3.3; 5.6.1; 6.3.5; 6.4.7; and 7.3.3. William Whiston, Trans., *The Works of Josephus* (Peabody: Hendrickson, 1987), Libronix e-book.

[79] Philo, *Flaccus*, 1.

[80] Josephus *Jewish Wars*, 6.8.6.

Unfortunately, this national/religious zeal (cf. Jn. 11:50-51) spilled over against the Christians as well.[81] They persecuted Christians in Jerusalem and Palestine (Acts 7:57; 9:1-2; 12:2; 1 Cor. 15:9) and elsewhere (Acts 13:50).

The Roman Emperor Nero also persecuted the Christians from A.D. 64 to 68, blaming them for a fire that damaged or destroyed much of Rome. Tradition says that Paul died under this persecution. The Emperor Domitian (A.D. 81-96) instituted emperor worship, proclaiming himself to be "God the Lord." When the Jews and Christians resisted, persecution resulted.

Segregation

Segregation because of religious and social practice characterized the relationship between Jews and Gentiles recorded in the New Testament. This was demonstrated in the lack of associations between Jews and Samaritans (Lk. 9:53-56; Jn. 4:9; cf. Ecclesiasticus 1:25-26)[82] and in the ceremonial separation between Jews and Gentiles (Jn. 18:28; Acts 10:28; 11:3; 22:21-23; Gal. 2:11-13). For a Jew, crossing the racial line meant to "defile" oneself—to violate one's religious beliefs (cf. Jn. 18:28; Acts 11:3; 21:17f). In fact, Barclay noted that if a Jew married a Gentile, the Jewish family would actually hold a funeral for the young man or woman.[83] The religious nature of the division between Jews and all other races created a nearly impenetrable barrier (though not all Jews followed this with prejudice).

Gentile writers, in turn, reacted to this with derision:

"...many educated Romans despised Jews because of their strange customs, proselytizing and exclusiveness ("haters of the human race") and because they showed no respect to Roman gods (Tacitus *Hist.* 5.8; Quintilian *Inst. Orat.* 3.7.21; Suetonius

---

[81] Christ warned of persecutions for His disciples (Mt. 24:9; Mk. 13:9-13).

[82] The Jews incurred their animosity for having destroyed the Samaritan temple on Mt. Gerizim in 128 B.C.

[83] Barclay, William. *The Letters to the Galatians and Ephesians*. Edinburgh: (The Saint Andrews Press, 1972), 125. Jews would not, therefore, serve in the military as this would prevent Sabbath keeping and possibly result in eating meat offered to idols. See Stambaugh, 51.

Claudius 25.4; Juvenal *Sat.* 14.96–104)."[84]

Even though the inclusion of the Gentiles as proselytes[85] existed in Judaism, the Jews often rejected the idea. This seems especially evident when the Gentiles were given preferential treatment over them (Lk. 4:25-29) or when the temple or rituals came into question (Acts 22:21-23; Gal. 2:11-13). A whole host of stipulations grew up during the intertestamental period to define and preserve distinct lines of separation between Jews and Gentiles beyond God's intent.[86]

In summary, separation from Gentiles came from the Jewish religious ideas of purity and holiness—imposed primarily to stay separate from idolatry. This was most seen in the rules separating Gentiles from the temple (with stringent warnings of death to trespassers) as well as the prohibitions against social interchange and intermarriage.

---

[84] Stanley E. Porter and Craig A. Evans, *Dictionary of New Testament Background : A Compendium of Contemporary Biblical Scholarship*, (Downers Grove: InterVarsity Press, 2000) Libronix e-book.

[85] One may consider God's election and separation of Israel from other nations as racist, but, in fact, His purpose was to preserve a holy people to Himself. This separation was temporary and never excluded those who sincerely wanted to convert. The Old Testament provided for the inclusion of Gentiles in the covenant promises under certain circumstances. See Julius Scott, Jr., "Gentiles and the Ministry of Jesus: Further Observations on Matt 10:5-6; 15:21-28," *Journal of the Evangelical Theological Society* 33 (June 1990): 165.

See also Arthur Lewis' handling of the laws for treating sojourners, intermarriage, and other nations in "Jehovah's International Love," *Journal of the Evangelical Theological Society* 15, (Spring 1972): 87-92. See also Walter Kaiser, "The Davidic Promise and the Inclusion of the Gentiles (Amos 9:9-15 and Acts 15:13-18): A Test Passage for Theological Systems," *Journal of the Evangelical Theological Society* 20 (June 1977): 97-111.

In addition, God intended that Israel be a model society from which He could reveal His nature and purposes to all nations (Is. 11:10; 49:6; 56:7; Mk. 11:17; Acts 13:46-48; Ro. 15:12), in order to provoke the inclusion of the Gentiles through the revelation of God's glory in the theocracy. (In fact, Paul mentions this very effect in reverse. The belief of the Gentiles should now provoke the Jews to jealousy and salvation (Ro. 11:11).)

[86] See Edersheim, *Sketches*, 31-32. Edersheim wrote: "So terrible was the intolerance, that a Jewess was actually forbidden to give help to her heathen neighbor, when about to become a mother (*Avod. S.* 2.1)!"

Prejudice

Prejudice appeared in the animosity between Jews and Samaritans (Lk. 9:53-56; Jn. 4:9), between Grecian Jews and Hebraic Jews (Acts 6:1) and between Jews and Gentiles (Acts 19:32-34; Titus 1:10-12). In Paul's epistle to the Romans, both Jews and Gentiles showed prejudice in their boasting and judgmental attitude (Ro. 2:1, 12, 17; 3:9; 11:13, 17-18).

However, despite impressions from the writings of several contemporary Latin authors who "poke fun at circumcision, abstinence from pork, and Sabbath observance," prejudice between Jews and Gentiles was not necessarily widespread. John Gager noted that the Roman authors' "jokes must be seen as part of their literary calling, which required them to resist the invasion of foreign cults and customs."[87] Flare-ups of racial prejudice were more often the result of specific outbreaks against oppressive overlords. As a whole, the Jews enjoyed a great deal of popularity among the various peoples with whom they settled, including the Romans. This is most evident by the existence of numerous God-fearers found in the ancient world and by the success of some Jews in proselytizing Gentiles.[88] Paradoxically, the Romans expelled the Jews from Rome no less than three times during the first century for various alleged infractions![89]

It may suffice to recognize that in any society of such ethnic diversity, there exists (along social, religious, and racial lines) segregation and prejudice as well as toleration and acceptance.

---

[87] John G. Gager, "Judaism as Seen by Outsiders," ed. Robert A. Kraft and George W. E. Nickelsburg, *Early Judaism and Its Modern Interpreters*, (Atlanta: Scholars Press, 1986), 110.

[88] See Scott, Jr., "The Cornelius Incident in the Light of Its Jewish Setting," *Journal of the Evangelical Theological Society* 34 (December 1991): 476-477. See Acts 2. Certainly Jewish culture also influenced the Greeks. Josephus mentions several accounts of conversion in *Antiquities* 18.81-84 and 20.17-48. For God-fearers see Acts 13:16.

[89] In AD 41, Claudius banned Jewish meetings (Dio Cassius *Roman History* 60.6.6). The Jews were also expelled under Tiberius (AD 19) because of a scandal involving the misappropriation of funds for the Jerusalem temple (Suetonius, *Life of Tiberius* 36).

Appendix G

An Overview of Jew/Gentile Racial Tensions Addressed in the New Testament

Jew/Gentile racial issues are frequently addressed in the New Testament[90] and this appendix has already examined several. However, one of the most significant groups that caused racial tension between Christian Jews and Christian Gentiles was the Judaizers. This appendix now turns to this group and the problems they caused.

The Judaizer Problem

A group, comprised largely of Jewish Christians, and known derogatively to Paul as the Judaizers,[91] taught the necessity of keeping the Law of Moses and Jewish customs before becoming a Christian. The hallmarks of their heresy consisted of requiring circumcision (Gal. 5:2, 11; 6:12-15), separation from Gentiles (Gal. 2:14-21), observance of the Mosaic Law (Gal. 3:2; 5:4) and certain festivals (Gal. 4:10), and apparent interest in being 'sons of Abraham' (3:6-29; 4:21-31)."[92] In Jerusalem, the Judaizers consisted of a small, but vocal minority of Pharisees (Acts 15:5), who were known for their strict adherence to the law.[93]

Theologically, the heresy was a threat to the truth of the gospel (Gal. 2:14-16) because justification comes by faith alone (Gal. 2:15-21). In practical terms, it instilled a sectarian spirit by separating Christian Jews from Christian Gentiles and by pressuring Gentile Christians to conform to the customs of Judaism. It thus worked against the reconciling nature of the gospel.

---

[90] A sampling of both direct and indirect verses includes: Lk. 4:25-29; 9:53-56; 19:7; Jn. 4:9; 18:28; Acts 6:1; 10:1-11:18; 11:3; 19:32-34; 22:21-23; 1 Cor. 12:13; Gal. 2:11-21; 3:28; 5:6-12; Eph. 2:11-22; 3:6, 8-9; 4:1-6; Col. 3:11-15; Titus 1:10-13; 1 Pt. 2:9-10.

[91] The name "Judaizers" is taken from Gal. 2:14 (ioudaizo). Paul had harsh words for the Judaizers (cf. Phil 3:2-4; Gal. 5:12). See the discussion in J. Becker, *The Faithfulness of God and the Priority of Israel in Paul's Letter to the Romans* in *The Romans Debate*, ed. Karl Donfried, *The Romans Debate* Revised and Expanded Edition (Peabody, Massachusetts: 1991), 328.

[92] Walt Russell, "Who Were Paul's Opponents in Galatia?" *Bibliotheca Sacra* 147 (July 1990): 331.

[93] F. F. Bruce captured the argument of the Judaizers (see Bruce, 180-181). See also an excellent assessment in Paul Minear, *The Obedience of Faith* (Eugene: Wipf and Stock Publishers, 1971), 73-74.

A controversy erupted in A.D. 49 when the Judaizers came to Antioch and taught that a person must first become a Jew before becoming a follower of Christ (Acts 15:1-2). At stake was not only how the gospel was to be presented to the Gentiles—would they have to jump through all the hoops of Judaism?—but the very gospel itself, which is not dependent on works (Eph. 2:8-10). The disagreement between Paul and the Judaizers resulted in the meeting at Jerusalem with the apostles and elders (Acts 15). The conclusion of the council sought to respect both Jews and Gentiles, thus preventing any hindrance for members of either group to come to Christ (Acts 15:19-21). The spread of the gospel among both Jews and Gentiles was taken into account and balanced, especially with respect to the sensibilities of the Jews.[94]

Galatians and the Judaizers

Paul's letter to the Galatians expressed astonishment that the Galatians had deserted the teachings of the gospel to follow the ritual law of the Judaizers (Gal. 1:6-10). Paul soundly rebuked the Galatians for abandoning the truth of the gospel—the truth that "a man is not justified by observing the law, but by faith in Jesus Christ" (Gal. 2:16).

As part of his argument, Paul recited an incident in which he had rebuked[95] Peter for compromising the gospel in a similar way. While at Antioch, Peter had eaten with Gentiles, but when a group of Judaizers came from Jerusalem (seemingly with authority from James), Peter separated himself from the Gentiles. Other Jews, including Barnabas, joined Peter's hypocrisy.

---

[94] The other commitment made by Paul at the Jerusalem council was to "remember the poor" (Gal. 2:20). Out of this request came Paul's passion to gather an offering from the Gentiles to the Jewish poor in Jerusalem. See Acts 24:17; Ro. 15:26; 1 Cor. 16:3-4; and 2 Cor. 8-9.

A decade or so after the Jerusalem council's decision, Paul had harsh words for the Judaizers who had evidently influenced the Philippians by their heresy (Phil 3:2-4; cf. Gal. 5:12). Paul derided the Judaizers as the "concision"— mutilators of the flesh (Phil. 3:2).

[95] Paul's words of rebuke to Peter includes the harsh terms *anthistemi* (set against) and *kategnosmenos* (know against; blame based on the act itself) in Gal. 2:11.

Paul not only addressed this as a threat to the truth of the gospel (Gal. 2:14-16), but he also expressed his concern over the resultant separation between Jewish Christians and Gentile Christians (Gal. 2:12). Often buried in the theological discussion of this passage is the segregation that took place. Further, the separation of the Jewish Christians from the Gentile Christians must have had a negative impact on the self-esteem of the Gentile Christians. Consequently, the Judaizers posed a real threat to the reconciliation of the races.

Paul's Epistle to the Romans and the Judaizers

The Judaizer problem may very well have been on Paul's mind as he wrote to the Romans. He wrote shortly after Emperor Claudius had expelled the large Jewish community (numbering perhaps 40,000 to 60,000) from Rome, "since they were continually making disturbances fomented by Chrestus" (a possible reference to Christ).[96] J. Dunn commented that this community:

> "...was both influential in Rome and deeply despised, not to say hated, by the most influential voices of Roman intelligentsia. This was partly because of its sheer size, partly because of the preferential treatment they had received from Julius Caesar and Augustus, and, probably more importantly, because of the numbers of Gentiles who were attracted to Judaism."[97]

The Roman authorities made a *racial response* to the disturbances by expelling the entire Jewish community (especially when only a portion was probably involved in the unrest). However justified the Roman authorities were for maintaining civil order, they targeted an entire ethnic group at Rome.[98]

---

[96] Estimates of Jews at Rome range from 10,000 to 60,000. See Leon Morris, *The Epistle to the Romans*, (Grand Rapids: Eerdmans, 1995), 4, n. 10. See Josephus, *Antiquities* 17.300-301 and *Jewish Wars* 2.80-81. Seutonius *Claudius* 25.4.

[97] Hawthorne, 839.

[98] Nero succeeded Claudius as the Roman emperor in AD 54. At this change in emperorship the edict would no longer be in force and these Jews could return to Rome without hindrance. Thus, the Bible records in Acts 18:2 that the Jewish

In constructing his epistle to the Romans, Paul may have recognized a very real threat to the gospel in the circumstances surrounding the recent banishment of the Jews from Rome. There would naturally be a heightened sense of racial division and residual animosity as the Jews returned, since they would find the leadership of the Church in Gentile hands. This could make the Jewish Christians more zealous for Jewish customs and segregation and therefore more sympathetic to the message of the Judaizers. If the "gospel" of the Judaizers had not preceded Paul to Rome, it would eventually get there (cf. Ro. 16:17-18).[99]

Paul mentioned those who slandered him (Ro. 3:8) and those who "cause divisions and put obstacles in your way" (Ro. 16:17)—earmarks of the Judaizers.[100] But most importantly, Paul's letter to the Romans seeks to level the relationship of Jews and Gentiles in Christ and reconcile the two factions—thus *preventing* a hostile environment ripe for the heresy of the Judaizers. The merging of dissimilar cultures and backgrounds would naturally cause friction and inevitably raise "questions as to Jewish and Christian identity."[101] This

---

Christian, Aquila, was expelled from Rome. Later we find him back in Rome (Ro. 16:3) when Paul wrote his letter to the Romans.

[99] Perhaps the Jewish Christians returning to Rome several years after the expulsion of Claudius may have brought it with them. Thomas Schreiner wrote: "He knew that doubts and questions had surfaced in the Roman congregations about his gospel, but he did not yet face full-fledged opponents. These apprehensions about Paul's teaching in Rome could be alleviated if his gospel were thoroughly explained, particularly on issues relating to Jews and Gentiles." See Thomas Schreiner, *Romans* (Grand Rapids: Baker Book House, 1998) 21. All Rome would know that Paul was "not ashamed" of the gospel!

[100] Another earmark of the Judaizers was their boasting about "your flesh"—the number of Gentiles they could get circumcised. Paul responded that he did not boast "except in the cross of the Lord Jesus Christ" (Gal. 6:13-14). The Greek word for "boasting" and its cognates appeared in contexts where Paul dealt with the prejudice of the Judaizers or spoke regarding racial reconciliation, especially in Romans and Corinthians (Ro. 2:17f; 3:27-31; 11:18; 15:17; 1 Cor. 1:22-31; 2 Cor. 11:12-30; cf. Jer. 9:24 LXX.), and also in the critical passage in Eph. 2:8-22. Boasting about one's race is an obvious characteristic of racial prejudice.

[101] J. Dunn, *Letter to the Romans*, ed. G. Hawthorne, R. Martin, D. Reid, *Dictionary of Paul and His Letters*, (Downers Grove: IVP, 1993), 839. He states, "This alone is sufficient to explain some of the characteristic elements and the message of the letter [to the Romans]: for example, 'who/what is a

could be fuel for the Judaizer's match, and Paul sought to avoid disunity through the reconciliatory message of the gospel. Thus, at least part of Paul's goal in writing his epistle was to avoid the past problems and reconcile the races.[102]

The Judaizers and Racial Problems in Acts

The Book of Acts followed the steady movement of the gospel message not only out from Jerusalem, but also away from Judaism and Jewish culture (cf. Acts 21:19-20). First was the promise that God "will pour out his Spirit on all flesh" (Acts 2:17). Then, confirmation of the Spirit came on a) the Samaritans (who had one foot in Judaism and one foot through intermarriage in the Gentile world; Acts 8:4-25); b) the Godfearers of Cornelius' household (who were Gentiles following many Jewish practices; Acts 10:1-11:18); and finally, c) on the Gentiles of Antioch (who practiced neither circumcision nor Jewish customs; Acts 11:19-30; 15:1-35). The Jerusalem Council convened to address directly the dispute between the Judaizers and Paul and Barnabas (Acts 15:1-2). The outpouring of the Holy Spirit on the Gentiles, coupled with Paul and Barnabas' report of the "miraculous signs and wonders" among the Gentiles, provided overwhelming proof that Gentiles did not have to first become Jewish proselytes before

---

Jew?' (Rom 2:25-29); who are 'the elect of God'? (Rom 1:7; 8:33; 9:6-13; 11:5-7, 28-32); and the climactic position of Romans 9-11 and Romans 15:8-12."

[102] In this case, it is not necessary for us to identify factionalism at Rome, only that it *could* occur. This purpose could also explain such major chapters as Ro. 2:17-3:31 (equal basis of Jews and Gentiles in Christ); Ro. 14 (where the "weak and the strong"—Jews and Gentiles respectively—are not to impose their consciences on each other). Chapter 16 shows the house churches divided among Jews and Gentiles. Further, Paul couches all his theological discussion in terms of the Jew/Gentile situation. And his diatribe is designed to unite Jews and Gentiles. See D. F. Watson, *Diatribe*, ed. G. Hawthorne, R. Martin, and D. Reid, *Dictionary of Paul and His Letters* (Downers Grove: InterVarsity Press, 1993), 213-214. See also Michael Goulder, *The Pauline Epistles* in Robert Alter and Frank Kermode, *The Literary Guide to the Bible*, (Cambridge: Harvard University Press, 1987), 497. T. W. Manson, *St. Paul's Letter to the Romans*, in *The Romans Debate*, 4, wrote: "Romans is the calm and collected summing-up of Paul's position as it had been hammered out in the heat of controversy during the previous months."

becoming Christians. They concluded that grace and faith—not circumcision—determined salvation (Acts 15:11). Thus, ceremonial law was rendered an unnecessary "yoke" (Acts 15:10). The decision of the Jerusalem council did not end the controversies, however, but it did lay the groundwork from which the gospel would spread in a more balanced way for both Jews and Gentiles. Thus, in his methodical manner, Luke showed us that salvation was extended to all—both Jew and Gentile. One by one the barriers of racial separation were torn down.

A further point to all this discussion is that the Judaizers were not only a significant movement in First Century Christianity, but also an indication of the resistance of Judaism against Hellenization. The Judaizer problem has largely been ignored as evidence of the opposite poles of Judaism and Hellenism. The resistance of the Judaizers was a "hold over" of the same resistance that existed in the Jewish community against the pressure of Hellenization. As misinformed as they were, the Judaizers sincerely intended to keep a separate, holy people in honor of God (albeit according to the old rules).

Ephesians and Racial Reconciliation

Perhaps a final word on racial reconciliation is in order and the keynote passage regarding this is Ephesians 2:11-22. Here Paul states that the "dividing wall of hostility" that was mutually erected by Jews and Greeks was destroyed in Christ. In His death the racial enmity of this age also died, for we died with Him. The resulting new man exists as part of the future humanity of the new creation age, where ethnicity remains, but racial animosity has ended.

Summary and Conclusion

Comprehending the multi-faceted conditions of the Jew/Gentile relationship contributes greatly to the background and understanding of the First Century situation and of the New Testament. It informs us of several important groups and many events—locally in Palestine and empire-wide. It plays an important role in understanding the growth of the fledgling Church and many early problems and challenges it faced. But perhaps most importantly, it shows how the Jewish and Gentile Christians struggled to overcome the racial walls of separation long entrenched in the Mediterranean world.

At Caesarea and Antioch, the eschatological Spirit had marked the Gentiles as members of the new community without requiring them to first keep Jewish rituals and customs. Further, where the Law had separated Jews and Gentiles, and where Gentiles had once been "aliens and strangers" from the covenants and patriarchs, now, through Christ, they were united together into "one new man" (what Dodd called a "supra-national society"). Christianity provided a solution through the formation of a third group—yes, born out of Judaism, but ultimately neither Jew nor Greek (Gal. 3:28)—that offered an alternative to the existing racial divisions.[103] Here lies the Christian basis for racial reconciliation: our identity no longer lies in racial status, but in our identity in Christ.

Despite how the Judaizers tried to rebuild the wall that Christ had torn down, the gospel of unity persisted. "There is no difference" (Ro. 3:22-23; 10:12-13) Paul would proclaim. No matter what race one hails from, all are united in Christ the same way.

---

[103] See Ro. 2:28-29; 9:6; Eph. 2:15; 1 Pt. 2:9.

Bibliography

Baker, G. W., W. L. Lane, and J. R. Michaels. *The New Testament Speaks.* New York, 1969.

Barclay, William. *The Letters to the Galatians and Ephesians.* 2nd ed. Edinburgh: The Saint Andrew Press, 1972.

Barnet, P. W. *Opponents of Paul.* In Gerald F. Hawthorne, Ralph P. Martin, and Daniel G. Reid, eds., *Dictionary of Paul and His Letters.* Downers Grove: InterVarsity Press, 1993.

Bauer, Walter. *A Greek-English Lexicon of the New Testament and Other Early Christian Literature.* Translated by William F. Arndt and F. Wilbur Gingrich. Chicago: The University of Chicago Press, 1957.

Bruce, F. F. *Paul, Apostle of the Heart Set Free.* Grand Rapids: Eerdmans, 1977.

Carson, D. A. and Douglass Moo. *An Introduction to the New Testament.* 2nd ed. Grand Rapids: Zondervan, 2005.

Dio, Cassius. *Roman History.* Vol. 60. Translated by Earnest Cary. Boston: Harvard University Press, 1927. http://penelope.uchicago.edu/Thayer/E/Roman/Texts/Cassius_Dio/60*.html (accessed March 25, 2008).

Dodd, C. H. *Christianity and the Reconciliation of the Nations.* London: The Camelot Press, 1952.

Donfried, Karl, gen. ed. *The Romans Debate.* Rev. ed. Peabody: Hendrickson, 1991.

Dunn, James. *Letter to the Romans.* In Gerald F. Hawthorne, Ralph P. Martin, and Daniel G. Reid, eds., *Dictionary of Paul and His Letters.* Downers Grove: InterVarsity Press, 1993.

_____. *The Partings of the Ways Between Christianity and Judaism and their Significance for the Character of Christianity.* Philadelphia: Trinity Press International, 1996.

Edersheim, Alfred. *Sketches in Jewish Social Life.* Sage Digital Library e-book.

Fong, Bruce W. "Addressing the Issue of Racial Reconciliation According to the Principles of Ephesians 2:11-22." *Journal of the Evangelical Theological Society* 38 no. 4 (December 1995): 565-580.

Gager, John G. *Judaism as Seen by Outsiders.* In Robert A. Kraft and George W. E. Nickelsburg, eds., *Early Judaism and Its Modern Interpreters.* Atlanta: Scholars Press, 1986.

Goulder, Michael. *The Pauline Epistles.* In Robert Alter and Frank Kermode, *The Literary Guide to the Bible.* Cambridge: Harvard University Press, 1987.

Green, Peter. *Hellenistic History and Culture.* Berkeley: University of California Press, 1993.

Gundry, Robert H. *A Survey of the New Testament.* 3rd ed. Grand Rapids: Zondervan, 1994.

Hengel, Martin. *The 'Hellenization' of Judea in the First Century after Christ.* Translated by John Bowden. Philadelphia: Trinity, 1989.

Hoch, C., Jr. "The Significance of the Syn-compounds for Jew-Gentile Relationships in the Body of Christ." *Journal of the Evangelical Theological Society* 25, no. 2 (June 1982): 175-183.

Jewett, Robert. *Romans: A Commentary.* Minneapolis: Fortress, 2007.

Josephus, Flavious. *Antiquities of the Jews.* Translated by William Whiston. Chicago: Thompson and Thomas, 1901. http://www.earlychristianwritings.com/text/josephus/josephus.htm (accessed March 25, 2008).

_____. *Jewish War.* Translated by William Whiston. Halifax: William Milner, 1850.

http://www.earlychristianwritings.com/text/josephus/josephus.htm (accessed March 25, 2008).

Kirk, J. Andrew. "Race, Class, Caste and the Bible." *Themelios* 10, no. 2 (Jan. 1985): 4-14.

Lewis, Arthur. "Jehovah's International Love." *Journal of the Evangelical Theological Society* 15, no. 2 (Spring 1972): 87-92.

Longenecker, Richard N. *The Acts of the Apostles.* In Frank E. Gaebelein, *The Expositor's Bible Commentary*, Vol. 9. Grand Rapids: Zondervan, 1981.

_____. Paul, *Apostle of Liberty: The Origin and Nature of Paul's Christianity.* Grand Rapids, Baker, 1980.

Madvig, D. "The Missionary Preaching of Paul: A Problem in New Testament Theology" *Journal of the Evangelical Theological Society* 20, no. 2 (June 1977): 147-155.

Mercer, Larry. "A Biblical and Cultural Study of the Problem of Racism." *Bibleotheca Sacra* 153, no. 609 (Jan. 1996): 87-103.

Moore, Thomas. "'To the End of the Earth': The Geographical and Ethnic Universalism of Acts 1:8 in Light of Isaianic Influence on Luke." *Journal of the Evangelical Theological Society* 40, no. 3 (September 1997): 389-399.

Morris, Leon. *The Epistle to the Romans.* Grand Rapids: Eerdmans, 1995.

Picirilli, Robert E. *Paul the Apostle.* Chicago: Moody Press, 1986.

Rapinchuk, Mark. "Universal Sin and Salvation in Romans 5:12-21." *Journal of the Evangelical Theological Society* 42, no. 3 (Sept. 1999): 427-441.

Reasoner, Mark. *The Strong and the Weak: Romans 14:1-15:13 in Context.* Cambridge: Cambridge University Press, 1999.

Robertson, A. T. *Epochs in the Life of Paul: A Study in the Development in Paul's Career.* New York: Charles Scribner's Sons, 1937.

Bibliography

Russell, W. "Insights from Postmodernism's Emphasis on Interpretive Communities in the Interpretation of Romans 7." *Journal of the Evangelical Theological Society* 37, no. 4 (1994) 511-527.

Schreiner, Thomas. *Romans*. Grand Rapids: Baker Book House, 1998.

Scott, J. Julius Jr., "Gentiles and the Ministry of Jesus: Further Observations on Matt 10:5-6; 15:21-28." *Journal of the Evangelical Theological Society* 33, no. 2 (June 1990): 161-169.

_____. "The Cornelius Incident in the Light of Its Jewish Setting." *Journal of the Evangelical Theological Society* 34, no. 4 (December 1991): 475-484.

Suetonius, C. Tranquillus. *The Lives of the Twelve Caesars*. Translated by Alexander Thomson. New York: R. Worthington 1883. http://www.fordham.edu/HALSALL/ANCIENT/suetonius-claudius-worthington.html (accessed March 25, 2008).

Stambaugh, John and David Balch. *The New Testament in Its Social Environment*. Library of Early Christianity, edited by Wayne Meeks. Philadelphia: The Westminster Press, 1986.

Stendahl, Krister. *Paul Among Jews and Gentiles*. Philadelphia: Fortress Press, 1976.

Stifler, James. *The Epistle to the Romans*. Chicago: Moody Press, 1983.

Stott, John. *The Message of Acts: The Spirit, the Church and the World*. Downers Grove: InterVarsity Press, 1990.

Wilson, Marvin. *Our Father Abraham: Jewish Roots of the Christian Faith*. Grand Rapids: Eerdmans, 1989.

Index of Scripture Verses

Genesis
15:6 *37*

Exodus
20:13-15 *85*
20:17 *85*

Leviticus
19:18 *84, 85*

Deuteronomy
5:7-21 *87*
5:17-19 *85*
5:21 *85*
6:4-5 *84*
31:24-26 *46*

Job
4:8 *86*

Psalm
126:5 *86*

Proverbs
22:8 *86*

Ecclesiastes
11:4 *86*

Isaiah
11:10 *112*
45:22 *27*
49:6 *112*
56:7 *112*

Jeremiah
9:24 *117*

Hosea
8:7 *86*
10:12 *86*

Amos
9:9-15 *112*

Matthew
2:1-12 *106*
3:7 *108*
4:15 *108*
8:5-13 *106*
10:5-6 *106, 112*
10:18 *13, 106*
12:14-21 *106*
15:21-28 *106, 112*
16:1-12 *108*
21:13 *106*
21:40-46 *106*
22:8-10 *106*
22:23 *108*
22:36-40 *84*
24:9 *13, 106, 111*
28:19 *13, 106*
28:19-20 *35*

Mark
7:14-15 *106*
7:19 *106*
11:17 *112*
13:9-13 *111*

Luke
4:25-29 *112, 114*
9:53-56 *111, 113, 114*
19:7 *114*

John
4:9 *111, 113, 114*
10:16 *106*
11:50-51 *111*
13:34 *85*
13:34-35 *82*
18:28 *111 (2x), 114*

Acts
1:8 *13 (2x), 116 (3x)*
2 *35*
2:17 *118*
2:17-3:31 *118*
5:17 *108*
6:1 *113, 114*
7:57 *111*
8:1-3 *109*
8:1-3 *109*
8:27 *35*
9:1-2 *109, 111*
9:9-13 *35*
9:15 *35*
10 *35, 108*
10:1-11:18 *1014, 118*
10:28 *35, 111*
10:44 *35*
11 *35*
11:3 *111 (2x), 114*
11:15 *35*
11:19-30 *118*
12:1-19 *109*
12:2 *111*
13:1 *36*
13:16 *113*
13:50 *111*
13:46-48 *112*
15 *12, 35 (2x)*
15:1-2 *12, 115, 118*
15:1-35 *118*

Index of Scripture Verses

(**Acts** Cont.)
15:5 *11, 16, 114*
15:10 *118*
15:11 *118*
15:13-18 *112*
15:19 *37*
15:19-21 *12*
15:21 *107*
15:23 *16*
15:36 *37*
16 *118*
17:6 *4*
17:26-28 *28*
17:28 *108*
18:2 *4 (3x), 116*
18:6 *36*
18:6 *37*
19:21 *15, 76*
19:32-34 *113, 114*
20:24 *33*
21:17f *111*
21:19-20 *118*
22:21-23 *111, 112, 114*
22:25-29 *24, 108*
23:6 *108 (2x)*
24:17 *12, 115*
26:5 *109*
26:15-18 *36*
28:2 *105*
28:28 *37*

Romans
1-2 *38*
1:7 *13, 117*
1:1-17 *2, 68-72*
1:10-13 *15, 76*
1:12-16 *8*
1:14 *64*
1:14-17 *1, 7*
1:16 *1*
1:17 *20, 37*

1:18 *22*
1:18-20 *25*
1:18-22 *26*
1:18-11:36 *2, 70-72*
1:18-2:1 *8*
1:19-32 *25*
1:29 *20*
1:32 *20*
2-3 *3*
2:1 *19, 20, 21, 22, 26, 113*
2:1-6 *55*
2:1-29 *26*
2:2 *27*
2:5 *20*
2:6-10 *26*
2:9-10 *7*
2:11 *27, 37*
2:12 *19, 20, 72, 113*
2:12-24 *14*
2:13 *20*
2:16 *16*
2:17 *20, 23, 38, 113*
2:17-18 *19*
2:17-24 *55*
2:17-3:31 *14*
2:21 *21*
2:23 *23*
2:25 *38*
2:25-29 *13, 26*
2:28-29 *120*
3 *38, 41, 84*
3-4 *37*
3:4 *27*
3:5 *20, 23, 28*
3:9 *19, 20, 21, 23, 28, 113*
3:10 *20*
3:19 *23, 27, 28*
3:19-20 *81*
3:20-22 *20*
3:21 *16*

3:21-30 *3, 7*
3:22-23 *23*
3:22-25 *27*
3:23 *20*
3:25-26 *20*
3:26 *27*
3:27 *3, 19, 21, 23, 27*
3:28 *27*
3:8 *14, 16*
3:9 *8, 63*
3:9-20 *25*
2:17 *117*
3:8 *117*
3:13-18 *26*
3:19 *8, 26, 63*
3:19-20 *38*
3:20 *28, 37, 81*
3:21 *80*
3:21-25 *43*
3:22 *28, 38*
3:22-23 *120*
3:26 *37*
3:27-30 *55*
3:27-31 *117*
3:28 *80*
3:29 *28*
3:29-30 *7, 27*
3:31 *14*
4 *37*
4:2 *19, 21, 23*
4:3 *20*
4:5-6 *20*
4:9 *20*
4:11 *20*
4:13 *20*
4:13-15 *31*
4:15 *37, 38, 81 (2x)*
4:16 *28, 38*
4:17-18 *37*
4:22 *20*
4:24 *20*
5-11 *33*

(Romans Cont.)	7:15-23 *38*	9:19 *55*
5:1 *35*	7:25 *96*	9:22 *55*
5:1-11 *64*	8 *37, 52*	9:23-24 *29*
5:7 *20*	8:1 *8, 19, 29, 96*	9:24 *56*
5:9 *43*	8:1-2 *31*	9:27-30 *29*
5:10-11 *43*	8:1-4 *45*	9:28 *20*
5:12 *23, 28*	8:2 *46, 52, 64, 82*	9:30-31 *20*
5:12-15 *26*	8:3 (2x) *46*	9:30-33 *56*
5:12-19 *43*	8:4 *20*	9:31 *16*
5:13 *37, 81*	8:5 *53*	9:32 *56*
5:17-19 *20*	8:10 *20, 52*	10:1 *63*
5:18 *23, 28, 38, 81*	8:12 *64*	10:1-3 *56*
5:18-19 *35*	8:12-17 *96*	10:3-6 *20*
5:20 *37, 81*	8:13 *53, 95*	10:4 *3, 16, 29, 31, 46,*
5:20-21 *44*	8:15 *29*	*56, 64, 82*
5:21 *20, 26*	8:17 *29, 96*	10:6-7 *56*
6-8 *44, 49, 53*	8:18-11:36 *29*	10:10 *20*
6:1 *16, 37, 44*	8:20 *26*	10:11-13 *29*
6:2 *44*	8:28 *1*	10:12 *30, 56*
6:3-4 *50, 91*	8:28-30 *29*	10:12-13 *30, 120*
6:4 *93*	8:29-30 *55*	10:16 *56*
6:4-5 *50, 91*	8:30 *50, 91*	10:16-17 *29*
6:5-8 *50, 91*	8:31 *1*	10:18 *29*
6:11 *50, 91, 95, 96*	8:31-39 *45*	10:18-19 *92*
6:11-13 *53*	8:32 *29*	11:1 *44, 56, 100, 115*
6:13 *20, 50, 91*	8:33 *13, 117*	11:1-4 *48*
6:14-15 *16*	8:33-34 *8*	11:5-7 *13, 117*
6:15 *37, 44*	9-11:10 *55*	11:6 *27*
6:16 *20*	9:6 *120*	11:11 *44, 56, 102, 112*
6:18-20 *20*	9:3 *63*	11:11-25 *6*
6:19 *53*	9:3-8 *105*	11:12 *102*
7 *37*	9:4-5 *111*	11:13 *19, 21, 113*
7:4 *31, 46, 82*	9:5 *24*	11:14 *102*
7:4-6 *42, 91*	9:6 *55*	11:17 *19*
7:6 *45, 82 (2x)*	9:6-9 *29*	11:17-18 *21, 113*
7:7 *42*	9:6-13 *13, 117*	11:17-20 *3*
7:7-9 *46*	9:11 *56*	11:17-24 *29*
7:7-25 *46, 63, 81*	9-11 *3, 13, 92, 117*	11:18 *19, 117*
7:7-8:4 *53*	9:12 *29, 56*	11:19-20 *19*
7:12 *20, 82*	9:13 *29*	11:20 *21*
7:13 *44*	9:14 *44, 55*	11:20-21 *56*
7:14 *63*	9:16 *29*	11:25 *56, 102*

Index of Scripture Verses

(Romans Cont.**)**
11:25-26 *8*
11:26 *56*
11:28-32 *13, 117*
11:32 *71*
11:32 *8, 29, 30 (3x), 56*
11:33-36 *56, 102*
11:36 *23, 30*
12 *4*
12:1-15:13 *2, 70-72*
12:3 *19, 21*
12:5 *21*
12:9 *19, 21*
12:13 *20*
12:16 *20*
13 *4, 23*
13:1-7 *23*
13:8-10 *85*
13:9 *21*
13:13 *19, 21*
14 *4*
14:1 *21, 60*
14:1-4 *19, 21*
14:1-15:13 *2, 22*
14:9 *21*
14:13 *14, 21*
14:13-17 *19, 21*
14:13-23 *21*
14:13-15:1 *84, 87, 88*
14:14 *64*
14:19 *21*
14:20 *14, 64*
15 *115*
15:1-9 *21*
15:6 *59*
15:6-12 *60*
15:7 *6, 34*
15:7-8 *6*
15:8 *8*
15:8-12 *13, 30, 117*
15:12 *112*

15:14-33 *2, 68-72*
15:16 *37*
15:17 *117*
15:19 *15*
15:19-21 *115*
15:23 *4, 15, 76*
15:23-24 *76*
15:23-28 *5, 15*
15:25-26 *15*
15:25-28 *76*
15:26 *12, 115*
15:28 *15*
15:30-32 *17 (2x)*
15:31 *42*
16 *2, 4, 69-72, 76*
16:3 *4 (2x)*
16:3-5 *4*
16:7 *4*
16:10 *4*
16:11 *4*
16:17 *14, 16, 19, 22, 76, 117*
16:17-18 *17, 117*
16:25-26 *16*

1 Corinthians
1:18-2:5 *16*
1:22-31 *117*
1:23 *48*
1:23-24 *40*
1:30 *96*
8 *88*
9:11 *86*
12:13 *114*
15:9 *111*
15:12 *95*
15:22 *96*
15:33 *108*
15:35 *95*
15:56 *46*
16:3-4 *12, 115*

2 Corinthians
3:17 *64*
5:1-10 *95*
5:16 *96*
5:17 *39, 96*
5:21 *96*
8-9 *12, 115*
9:6 *96*
10:16 *76*
11:12-30 *117*

Galatians
1:6-10 *115*
1:6-3:14 *16*
1:11-12 *16*
1:11-5:14 *9*
2:1-2 *16*
2:3-5 *16*
2:6 *37*
2:7-9 *37*
2:11 *115*
2:11-13 *111, 112*
2:11-14 *108*
2:11-21 *13, 16, 49, 92, 107, 114*
2:12 *116*
2:14 *11, 12, 16*
2:14-16 *12, 114, 115*
2:14-21 *11, 16, 114*
2:15 *14*
2:15 *37*
2:15-21 *12, 114*
2:16 *115*
2:17 *37, 44*
2:20 *20, 115*
3:2 *11, 114*
3:3 *37*
3:6-9 *37*
3:6-29 *11, 114*
3:11 *37*
3:13 *49, 92*

3:14-18 *37*
3:19 *37*
3:21 *42*
3:24 *45*
3:26-28 *38*
3:26-29 *49, 92*
3:28 *38*
3:28 *97, 114, 120*
4:8-11 *38*
4:10 *11, 38, 114*
4:21-31 *11, 114*
5:2 *11, 114*
5:4 *11, 114*
5:6 *38*
5:6-12 *114*
5:11 *114*
5:12 *13, 16, 115*
5:13-14 *84*
5:16 *37*
5:17 *38*
5:24 *93*
6:7-9 *86*
6:11-16 *9, 16*
6:12-15 *11, 114*
6:13 *25, 38 (2x)*
6:13-14 *117*
6:15 *38*
6:15-16 *49, 92*

Ephesians
1:3 *51, 91*
2:6 *51, 91*
2:8-9 *39*
2:8-10 *12, 115*
2:8-22 *117*
2:11-14 *29*
2:11-22 *13, 114, 119*
2:11-3:12 *9*
2:11-3:13 *39*
2:12 *39*
2:13-16 *49, 92*
2:14 *13, 39, 105*
2:15 *39, 120*
2:20-23 *93*
3:6 *16, 114*
3:8-9 *114*
4:1-6 *114*
4:28 *53*

Philippians
3:2 *13, 115*
3:2-4 *13, 16, 115*
3:5 *108*
3:14 *96*
3:19-20 *95*
3:24 *16*

Colossians
1:19-22 *40*
1:24-29 *40*
2:2-23 *94*
2:9-10 *96*
2:11-12 *94*
3:1-3 *95*
3:5 *95*
3:9-11 *40*
3:11 *105*
3:11-15 *114*

1 Thessalonians
2:14-16 *40*
4:13 *94*
5:10 *94*

1 Timothy
2:3-7 *40*
3:16 *40*

2 Timothy
2:11-12 *94*
2:14 *94*

Titus
1:10-12 *113*
1:10-13 *114*
1:12 *108*

1 Peter
2:9 *120*
2:9-10 *114*

1 John
4:19-21 *85*

Index of Scripture Verses